TIE DYED:
Avoiding Aquarius

Also by Kathie Farnell

Duck and Cover: A Nuclear Family

TIE DYED:
Avoiding Aquarius

Kathie Farnell

Artemis Media Project
Foley, Alabama 2021

Artemis Media Project
Foley, Alabama 36535
artemismedia.org

Cover Design: Kathie Farnell
Production: Jan Pruitt
Author Photo: Judith Howard
Frowny Face: Vilmos Varga/Shutterstock.com
Background: PinkCactus/Shutterstock.com

Cataloging-in-Publication data is available from
the Library of Congress
Library of Congress Control Number: 2022901392

ISBN: 978-0-578-33648-0
E-ISBN: 978-0-578-36036-2

For Jack, of course

Contents

Introduction

Even though it was the dawning of the Age of Aquarius, you still had to go to school.

The late Sixties and early Seventies has lingered in the public imagination as a hellhole of unbridled sex, drugs, war, violence and rock 'n' roll inevitably accompanied by a soundtrack of "All Along the Watchtower" (scenes from Viet Nam) or "Sympathy for the Devil" (rock concerts and/or riots.)

For me, the time period from 1967 to 1973 was probably like what somebody once wrote about the Hundred Years War—yes, it was a war, but that doesn't mean people were fighting nonstop.

During a time of frightening, ridiculous, and occasionally just plain weird change, families like mine still coped, however cluelessly, with mundane concerns.

At this point, our household consisted of me, my two younger brothers Ray and Clay (the names weren't supposed to rhyme but something happened), a fluffy black-and-white tomcat named Abicat, and my widowed mother, whose law degree wasn't doing much to help her earn our living. My grandmother, known as Granny to everybody but Mama, who called her Mrs. Farnell if forced to interact with her, wasn't technically part of our household once she died, but try telling her ghost that.

They say that if you can remember the Sixties, you missed the whole point. Nevertheless, here's what I remember about a time when everybody else was letting the sunshine in while I was fending off hippies, Folk Mass and Jeb Stuart Magruder.

Hemline

When I started tenth grade in 1967, Sidney Lanier High School had 1600 students. This number was due to decrease with the opening of the brand-new Jefferson Davis High School which would siphon off all the rich kids whose parents didn't want to send them to the Montgomery Academy. Meanwhile, entering Lanier was pretty much like walking into a full-scale riot. When I fought my way upstairs against the tidal wave of students running down, I had some sympathy for salmon trying to swim upstream. The school building itself was an enormous old pile, built in the 1920s, and resembled either a castle or a place the Russians take people to interrogate, depending on your mood.

The real live Sidney Lanier was known as "the poet of the Confederacy," so naturally the football team was named the Poets. Possibly in a reaction to their name, the team was extremely belligerent and usually won the state championship.

Anyone wandering into Lanier noticed that, although integration had been the law for more than ten years, the school was home to very few black students. Lanier was still fighting a rear-guard action against integration; the official policy seemed to waver between ignoring the black students in hopes they would leave, or issuing bizarre decrees that would ensure the black students thought all white people were crazy. For one thing, it had been decided that students would no longer take showers after PE.

I had PE first period. Do the math.

Logically, I should have had bigger things to worry about than spending the rest of the school day damp, rumpled, and, if I had had the misfortune to be playing softball, covered in dirt.

1

The news was full of Viet Nam, rioting, and drugs, not to mention the birth control pill, but at this juncture Lanier decided to concentrate on combating what it saw as the country's number-one menace, right up there with integration.

The mini-skirt.

At Lanier, it was pretty hard to be fashion forward. Some new style would come in, for example, culottes or what was billed as the skort: basically shorts covered with panels of fabric which would lead the uninitiated to conclude you were wearing a skirt. These new fashions were good for about two weeks; after the majority of girls had purchased one, the school would finally notice and decide, on no evidence, that the garment was actually a mini-skirt and therefore banned.

Things could have been worse. I could have been going to Catholic High.

My across-the-street neighbor, the annoying Patty Harris, had started Catholic at the same time I started Lanier, thanks to a loophole. Even though Patty was a year younger than me, the fact that Catholic started in ninth grade meant that she got to go around showing off about being in high school. To make matters worse, next year she would be going to tenth grade at Jeff Davis, at which time she would undoubtedly become completely insufferable. Meanwhile, the only comeuppance she got was the fact that she, like my best friend Annette DeSalvo, had to wear Catholic High uniforms.

These uniforms were, I was happy to see, extremely ugly. They featured plaid skirts in a length last seen in 1955 and voluminous tops which made the wearer look like a bag of laundry. They were probably, in fact, the Catholic Church's official substitute for the birth control pill.

Whenever Patty and I happened to be in Belk's looking at the rack of Singer Sew-Easy Dress Patterns, I would be sure to select one which showed a teen wearing a dress whose brevity meant that in real life she could never bend over. "Look at this," I would say happily. Patty would fume.

With Annette I had to be a little more circumspect. Besides, she didn't sew, so I was restricted to pointing out the latest short styles in magazines. Annette wasn't taking the fashion tyranny lying down.

Both she and Patty had suitably brief skirts, and in Annette's case skorts, for wearing in their leisure time, but Annette had decided that the school uniforms could be made wearable with a little adjustment. This involved rolling the top of the skirt up about her waist and then covering the resulting inner tube effect with the roomy uniform top. The stratagem would even work if one of the more evil nuns made the wearer kneel to see if the skirt would reach the floor. On the way down, you had merely to give the skirt's hem a hefty yank, and you'd be legal. Sadly, Annette had yet to figure out a way around the uniform saddle shoes.

The roll-up strategy had not originated with Annette; a variation played out daily at Lanier. The fashion-conscious student might roll her skirt up and, if challenged, surreptitiously yank the hem down, or an alternative might be pursued. This involved attracting the attention of one of the more dowdy teachers early in the day and securing an official ruling that your skirt was no shorter than the requisite two inches above the knee. Then, you went in the bathroom, unzipped the skirt, yanked it up under your armpits, and pinned it to your bra. This only worked with an overblouse, but it was better than nothing.

On top of the trauma of seeing my classmates in the bathroom with a mouthful of safety pins, I was exposed to a daily skirt dilemma at home. Whereas the school didn't think my skirts were long enough, Mama thought they were too long. The fact that I made most of my clothes meant, in her opinion, that I had not only the right but the duty to make sure I was the height of teen fashion.

Mama was able to keep up with what the other students were wearing since she always dropped me off at school on the way downtown to her job. After school let out, I would walk through the Lanier parking lot, cut through Sears, and meet Mama in the Sears parking lot, from which it was a straight shot home unless we went to the nursing home to visit Granny, who had been incarcerated there since suffering a fall earlier in the year. Following my father's death five years earlier, Mama, a trained attorney who had never passed the Alabama State Bar Exam, had had to support us by working as a legal secretary. The law firm had enough sense to know that it was getting a lawyer for the mere pittance it paid secretaries, so Mama's hours were pretty flexible, though she still had to stay late at the firm sometimes to correct somebody else's mistakes. If Mama was going to be late picking me up, I whiled away the time in Sears looking at fabrics and pattern books, occasionally purchasing a pattern captioned "Make it Tonight, Wear it Tomorrow!"

This pattern was always lying.

For one thing, Abicat had developed a consuming interest in sewing. About the time I got all the pattern pieces laid out on the floor, somebody would open the door and Abi would come bouncing in scattering patterns, material, and pins to the winds.

For another thing, Mama had also developed a consuming interest in sewing. We had her old 1920s model electric sewing machine, which always smelled like it was about to catch on fire and which I had to set up on the kitchen table, with Abicat crouching alertly underneath. The sewing machine was easy to use since it only had two settings, Forward and Reverse, and Mama had been adept with it, sewing her own maternity clothes so she could show up in court wearing something which didn't have bunnies printed all over it.

She didn't make her own clothes anymore, but she was always interested in what I was making, specifically my skirts.

I had tried explaining that the school would make life hell for anybody wearing a mini-skirt, but I don't think she really believed me. This was strange, because my youngest brother Clay was running right into the male equivalent of a mini-skirt ban at Williams School, where he was currently serving an indeterminate sentence. Williams was a sort of cross between a military academy and a reform school. Mama had scrimped to send Clay there, thinking that military discipline would free him of his bad habits of not talking enough and spending all his free time at the home of his best friend Bobby Dobbs.

At Williams, Clay had to wear a uniform and keep his hair unfashionably short. The result was that Clay, miserable, stopped talking altogether and was at Bobby Dobbs' house more often than Bobby Dobbs was. As for military discipline, all it had done was make Clay pay particular attention to the television news about draft dodgers fleeing to Canada. Ray, my other brother, was still at Cloverdale Junior High, at which the administration generally turned a blind eye to hair, but he refrained from taunting Clay either out of sympathy or because Clay could beat him up.

4

Meanwhile, my fashion dilemma was causing me some qualms. I realized Mama was trying to ensure that I would be popular at school, although short of turning into Cleopatra I was not going to be as popular as she had been. I mean, except for the hair I looked sort of like Twiggy, but that wasn't the same thing.

It seemed impossible to arrive at a compromise which would placate both Mama and the school skirt police. Finally, I had an idea. One morning I appeared at breakfast sporting my latest creation, an outfit featuring a skirt so short that I could have been mistaken for the Caucasian version of *Star Trek*'s Lt. Uhura, whose uniform skirt did not always cover her matching uniform undies.

Mama beamed. I got myself into the car with some difficulty and once at Lanier carefully unloaded myself and my armload of books and shuffled into the building, taking care to avoid the stairs. Then I slid into the bathroom, unpinned my skirt from my bra, and jerked the hem back down. The bathroom had a mirror. My skirt was now two inches above the knee.

I smiled.

Pot-Bellied Burglar

There was a burglar loose in the neighborhood. None of our doors would lock.

Our house had been built in 1920 by a guy who for some reason had allegedly then gone in the dining room and shot himself, so the atmosphere was always a little iffy at best.

Nevertheless, this should have been a good time at our house because finally there was enough room. Mama had settled a lawsuit, known far and wide as The Texas Case, that my father had been working on at the time of his death. This case involved an estate with a lot of money, and the heirs finally got fed up enough to call it quits and pay the lawyer. With the money, Mama had decided to remodel the attic so I could live in it.

On the one hand, it was great. I had my own bedroom, a sitting room, and a bathroom. On the other hand, there was no heat except what wafted up from the floor furnace, located dangerously at the foot of the stairs, and I was afraid to use the bathroom. In the daylight it was okay, but at night I had to stumble to the other end of the house to access it, passing the door to what was left of the actual attic in the process. The actual attic, in addition to being scary, was home to the attic fan, and this complicated our home security situation.

For the attic fan to work, it was necessary that the front door be open, leaving the flimsy screen door as the only thing standing between us and the Pot-Bellied Burglar.

This burglar, who had been heavily featured in the *Montgomery Advertiser*, was described as a white guy with a pot belly. That certainly narrows it down, I thought grimly, since out-of-shape white guys were pretty much everywhere you looked.

Our house wasn't secure but it was much roomier right now because Granny was still in the nursing home terrorizing the staff, none of whom agreed with her theory that she needed a chamber pot under her bed. Ray and Clay continued to share a bedroom since nobody knew when Granny might suddenly reappear and want her old room back.

Meanwhile, the burglar's rampage was the tip of the iceberg as far as crime went. Cloverdale, our neighborhood, had once been fairly peaceful with the exception of a notorious case in which a woman beat her husband to death with a feather duster.

A really big feather duster.

Those days were gone. Now people, with the exception of my family, were locking their doors. I tried to impress this upon Mama, stating that she should at least close the door, but she wasn't impressed. "I'm not scared of them," she said courageously, "them" being burglars, pot-bellied or otherwise.

I pointed out that they didn't check first to see if you were scared.

I was scared enough for both of us. Crime was big news. Lately there had been an epidemic of women being set upon and murdered on their way home from work. The fact that this was taking place in New Jersey wasn't much comfort. According to *Life* magazine, which was covering the situation intensively, if you got set upon and murdered there was no use screaming for help, because nobody wanted to get involved.

Instead, you had to take steps to protect yourself. One of *Life*'s scariest photo essays depicted a young woman's efforts to avoid being set upon. The first photo was a close-up of her lighting a cigarette. The caption read, "Lighting a cigarette which she could jam into an assailant's eye, Mary Louise begins the long walk to her car."

I didn't smoke. I wondered if I should start.

The second photo showed the same woman with a bunch of keys. The caption read "Gathering her car keys, Mary Louise prepares to use them like brass knuckles."

I didn't drive either.

I was literally losing sleep over the burglar scare, but I felt a little better after I finally figured out a way to at least secure the back door. Just inside that door was a laundry room with a washer and dryer which didn't work. Then there was a door to the kitchen. If I pulled out a kitchen drawer, it would jam the laundry room door so that it only opened a few inches, not enough for a pot-bellied burglar, or even a slim one.

It wasn't much, but at least I was doing my part.

My godmother, Miss Bonnie Terrell, wasn't much help as far as keeping up our morale. She was concerned, she said, about me and

Mama living by ourselves. This sounded a little unfair to Ray and Clay, but in fact on one occasion when Ray thought he heard a burglar, he and Clay had climbed out their window and run off, leaving me and Mama to our own devices.

The burglar had, happily, turned out to be our cat, but Abicat wasn't much of a morale booster either. He had a habit of suddenly crouching down on the screened porch and peering out into the darkness with an alarmed look on his face, occasionally swishing his tail. "What is it?" I would say nervously.

I never figured out if he had really seen anything, and if he had he wouldn't have been a whole lot of help. For a tomcat, he was completely nonviolent. The attic occasionally had mice; when we shut him up in there and urged him to deal with it, Abicat had merely curled up and taken a nap.

Fall droned on. Eventually it got too cold for the attic fan, so at least we could close the front door. Granny recovered her ability to walk to a certain extent and returned home to the great relief of the nursing home staff and patients. She was still unsteady on her feet, though, so if Mama happened to be going out for the evening, she would get Ella Harrison to keep an eye on Granny. Ella was a large, calm woman who didn't mind watching Granny since, as Ella put it, she was used to her.

One Saturday in November, I spent the night with Annette and Mama went off with Miss Bonnie to her daughter Lana's school play. As reported to me the following day, Mama had returned to find the house in an uproar and Ray and Clay excitedly reporting that the cops had been there. The police, Ella had said resignedly, had been called by a neighbor upon seeing a car occupied by a black man parked in front of our house. The black man in question was of course Ella's husband John, there to collect Ella little early. The police, when Mama contacted them to, as she put it, "get to the bottom of this," had been unrepentant, stating that Mama shouldn't refer to her neighbors as "senile old drunks," but should be glad someone was concerned about her safety since there were some dangerous characters abroad in the neighborhood. Mama was concerned that Ella, not to mention John, wouldn't want anything further to do with us, but Ella reassured her, saying that they needed the money and that they were used to police.

Mama said grimly that from now on, she would go pick Ella up. Granny's comment on the incident was "Pshaw."

Upon hearing the part about the dangerous characters, Miss Bonnie had urged Mama to get a gun, and in fact Mama had been sufficiently concerned to bring home one of the handguns left over from my father's unsuccessful career as a criminal defense lawyer. The fact that we didn't have any bullets and that nobody knew how to fire the thing wasn't all that important, said Mama, since the main idea was to scare the burglar long enough for us all to escape.

One evening a couple of weeks after the police incident, I heard an ominous thumping coming from the actual attic. I went downstairs in something of a hurry, narrowly missing landing on the floor furnace, to look for reinforcements. Clay had been last seen headed for Bobby Dobbs' house, Ray was watching *Lost in Space*, Mama was paying bills, and Abicat, I assumed, was taking a catnap.

Granny was in her room, muttering.

"I think there's somebody in the attic," I said. As I spoke, we all heard it. Ray suggested we get in the car and leave. Mama wasn't having any. She retrieved the handgun from under her bed. I had to admit this gun was pretty impressive. It was probably a Colt .45 or something; she had to use both hands to pick it up. Everybody except Granny headed upstairs, Ray in the rear.

Mama threw open the door to the attic. "Come outta there," she barked authoritatively, "with your hands up."

Clay appeared. He didn't have his hands up, since he was carrying Abicat.

"What," he said, sounding somewhat aggrieved.

He had, it developed, been back from Bobby's for some time, and had decided to while away the evening teaching Abicat to hunt mice. I asked if it had worked. He shrugged.

Just before I went to bed, it began raining heavily. I was relieved. No burglar, pot-bellied or otherwise, was going to get out in this downpour. With that comforting thought, I went to sleep.

Old Ladies

We were watching the Auburn-Alabama game when I expressed dissatisfaction with the quality of the crowd shots. "Why do they keep showing fat old ladies?" I thought this was a perfectly reasonable criticism, but Mama seemed offended. "I'm friends with a lot of fat old ladies," she said.

That was the trouble. Really, the only fat one I could think of was Mrs. Sears, but Mama did spend a lot of her rare free time taking care of old ladies. I counted. Mrs. Sears, Mrs. McAtee, Mrs. Rose, Mrs. Stacey, Mrs. Turner (who come to think of it was also fat), and worst of all Mrs. Krays. Mrs. Krays, who was inevitably referred to by my brothers and me as Mrs. Crazed, had a bad habit of calling at mealtimes to announce that she was unable to find her pocketbook. At least Mama refrained from driving over to conduct a search, but she was capable of spending fifteen minutes on the phone with the old lunatic going over all the places where the pocketbook might be.

The one thing these old ladies had in common besides being old was that they were all ingrates. Nothing Mama did seemed to satisfy them, but Mama didn't appear to notice. "We are put in this world to help others," she would say.

In that case, what were the others there for? I didn't get it.

I also thought it was odd that if she wanted to hang around with hypercritical old ladies, she hadn't just hung around Granny, since you couldn't get more hypercritical than that. It could be that Granny was too predictable; maybe Mama thought that one of these days she'd get an old lady to say "thank you."

Christmas seemed to bring out the worst in these old ladies and Mama spent a lot of time hauling them around to various stores so they could be sure of getting the very best prices on Christmas cards.

One evening Mama had just gotten off the phone after spending twenty minutes listening to Mrs. Krays' latest misadventure with her pocketbook, when the phone rang again. "I'll tell that old bat to shove her damn pocketbook if she ever finds it," I muttered, snatching up the receiver. It was Annette. Did I want to go look at Christmas lights with her and Nick Wallach?

This was an odd invitation. Nick's actual name was Nicole. She was a big bruiser of a girl; there was a rumor she was planning to try out for football. Annette always seemed kind of frightened of Nick, and I wasn't sure why she hung around with her, unless she was afraid not to. Apparently Annette was inviting me along as a bodyguard or witness or something and I was about to refuse, when she whispered that there was more at stake here than looking at a bunch of lights. "She's going to visit Nana," said Annette, "And we're taking her a bottle of Southern Comfort."

This was interesting. Nana was Nick's family's maid, long since retired, and Nick seemed to retain fond memories of her. More to the point, I loved Southern Comfort, though I wasn't exactly sure what was in it. It looked like wine but tasted like peach brandy with a lot of extra sugar. In fact, I wondered why nobody had ever thought of incorporating it into cake frosting. If Nana had a hospitable bone in her body, she would open up that Southern Comfort and pass it around.

"Sure," I said.

When Nick pulled up in her old Dodge, I prepared to climb in back, but Annette forestalled me by hopping out. "We can all sit in front," she announced. "Here, you sit next to Nick."

"Sheesh," I said, but I crawled in anyway. I had to admit Nick was pretty jovial, and she laughed raucously as she drove us through McGehee Estates, a subdivision which was home to many an over-the-top Christmas display, on the way to the black neighborhood where Nana lived. Finally we pulled up in front of a row of little wooden houses. I didn't know if Nick had checked first to see if Nana would be home, but there were Christmas lights in her front window and once we climbed the rickety porch steps and knocked on the door, she opened it promptly.

"Baby!" she greeted Nick, which was rather funny since Nick at this point was around a foot taller and 90 pounds heavier than Nana. I was sort of afraid Nick would pick her up.

Instead, Nick just grinned, said "Merry Christmas, Nana, I brought you something," and held out the gift-wrapped bottle.

"Look at that!" said Nana happily, tearing off the paper. "You brought Nana favorite drink!" Urging us to sit, she disappeared through a door. We sat on a faded couch beneath a picture of Jesus and one of Dr. Martin Luther King. I heard clinking sounds coming from what I assumed was the kitchen and in a moment Nana reemerged with a tray and glasses. "Merry Christmas!" Nana poured us all a generous serving, then set the bottle down on her coffee table next to the latest issue of *Jet*.

The more we drank, the more nostalgic Nick grew. "Nana," she said finally in rather a choked voice, "you were the only one who loved me."

Nana set her glass down. "Baby, Nana still love you."

I was concerned that Nick might become too drunk and emotional to drive and we'd have to depend on Annette, who couldn't drive a stick, to get us home, but finally Nick appeared to pull herself together and we stumbled down the steps, waving merrily.

"It's true," said Nick, on the drive home. "She loved me no matter what I did."

I nodded abstractedly. Libby and Lee had been our family maids. Lee had died three years ago, and Libby lived in Cleveland, from which we got an annual Christmas card. My relationship with Libby had been somewhat strained thanks to the fact that my brothers and I were fond of tormenting her with an artificial snake which we hid in places she was sure to look. Lee and I had, however, loved each other unconditionally; and even if we hadn't it would never have occurred to either one of us to ambush the other party with a fake snake. I sighed.

The next day, I found Mama in something of a quandary. It involved fish. She had driven Mrs. Sears to a house in Normandale where Mrs. Sears had purchased a number of very attractive tropical fish for an aquarium she was preparing as a Christmas present for her son. However, Mrs. Sears had not hooked up the aquarium heater correctly and the fish had all died. Now Mrs. Sears, ashamed to admit her negligence to the fish seller, wanted Mama to call the guy and pretend to want a batch of fish, which Mama would then pass along to Mrs. Sears.

This was, I thought, a no-brainer. Mama was always after us to tell the truth. After Mama's own mother died, she had been raised by her maiden aunt, for whom I had been named. Aunt Katherine was a school principal and a strict disciplinarian with a particular aversion to any conduct involving lying, being lazy, going barefooted, being inconsiderate, being late for meals, not practicing the piano enough, eating collards, listening to jazz, or using oilcloth instead of linen for a tablecloth. In fact, pretty much everything. There was no way Mama was going to tell a lie.

I was amazed when, later that day, I passed the phone in time to hear Mama say, "Oh, Mr. Tolliver, I admired your fish so much that I would like some for my own."

Now Mrs. Sears even had Mama lying for her. This was really getting out of hand. I shook my head as I passed into the dining room where I planned to search through the bureau drawer. This bureau was a sort of desk which served as a repository for interesting artifacts, like the newspaper with the headline "Nazis Quit," and a letter I had once found from Cammie, my father's first wife, who had written "I have long since forgiven you."

I was looking for Christmas cards, since we still had boxes of rather nice ones left over from the 1950s. The box I opened, however, proved to contain old letters. I was sort of interested, since I had never been exactly sure why my father had needed forgiving, but it turned out these letters were from Aunt Katherine, not Cammie. Aunt Katherine had died in 1960, but these letters went way back. They had in common the fact that most of them contained some veiled criticism of Mama for a shortcoming or omission. One of them was dated less than two months after my father had suffered his first heart attack. "It seems to me," wrote Aunt Katherine to Mama, "that it has been a while since I had a nice newsy letter from you." Mama had apparently started a reply. There was a sheet of Mama's stationary with "Christmas and I was just so exhausted" written at the top but then there wasn't any more. She must have misplaced the piece of paper before she could finish. I wondered briefly what Mama had intended to answer, but then I shrugged. Nothing would have made any difference.

On Christmas Eve, as we were sitting down to eat, the phone rang. "I'll get it," I said.

It was, of course, Mrs. Krays. Where was her pocketbook?

"Just a minute," I said. "I'll get Mama."

Granny's Ghost

Granny was dead. Try telling her that.

She had suffered another fall after the first of the year and had suddenly been admitted to the hospital. She died on a Saturday night. Mama had already arranged for Ella Harrison to come sit with Granny on Sunday morning while we went to church. Since the Harrisons didn't have a phone, Mama had gone to pick Ella up as planned. Ella greeted her with "Old Miss Farnell is dead, ain't she."

Mama, startled, asked how Ella knew. "Because," said Ella, "I dreamt about white sheets."

Trying to recover the conversational ball, Mama said that if Ella wanted to, she could come attempt to clean the house this morning. Or if she'd rather not—Mama's attempt to be diplomatic was interrupted by Ella, who was climbing into the car. "Don't you worry about me," she said reassuringly. "Dead people don't bother me. I sees them all the time."

Mama didn't report the exchange to me. As soon as she got home with Ella, we piled into the car and roared off to church. When we returned, Ella pulled Mama aside. "I heard Old Miss Farnell," she confided.

"WHAT?" said Mama.

Ella reported that she had been mopping when she heard Granny call for her.

"What'd you do?" asked Mama.

Ella had calmly gone to the door of Granny's room and asked "What you want, Miss Farnell?"

At that point, Ella had seen the covers of the bed stirring as if someone was trying to sit up. The voice came again. "Ella, help me!"

Ella, unable to offer anything in the way of aid, had gone back to mopping.

"If she keep on bothering y'all," said Ella cheerfully, "You gets a horseshoe and nails it upside down over the door. That'll fix her."

Mama, shaken, drove Ella home without mentioning the incident to me or my brothers. When Mama returned, she was surprised to see me sitting on the front steps, minus my coat but still in my church clothes.

I had been standing in front of the big mirror over the living room fireplace, frowning at my hair. Perhaps it was time to experiment with color.

At that point, I heard Granny call me. It was loud. In fact, it was so loud I started to answer. I got out "WHA—" before I remembered Granny was dead and that under no circumstances should she be calling me. I then went out in the yard.

Mama convinced me to come back inside, but the situation worried her.

She was on record as not believing in ghosts. Since Mama had had the misfortune of losing her entire nuclear family before she reached eighteen, she had said repeatedly that if there were such things as ghosts, by this time she would have seen at least a couple.

It was possible that Mama, who had grown up in a little village in Mississippi, had had more contact with ghosts than she wanted to acknowledge. For one thing, the big shadowy house where Mama had lived with Aunt Katherine sounded haunted. According to Mama, you would be sitting there and all the doors in the house would open by themselves. Then they would all close by themselves. Since she didn't officially believe in ghosts, Mama had had to blame the phenomenon on the Earth's magnetic field or something.

After Aunt Katherine died, Mama sold the house to Emil Dennis, who owned the village's store. The Dennis family had spent one night in the house, then promptly put it back on the market.

Our house in Montgomery might very well have been haunted by the time my parents moved in, since there was the persistent rumor that the original owner had committed suicide in the dining room, rather than going outside where he wouldn't have made a mess.

The dining room was dark and gloomy and I didn't like going in there, but I had always attributed the bad vibe to the fact that my parents used it for a home office and that the table was always piled with files. If the suicide guy was still around, though, he had never actually bothered me and had certainly never tried to strike up a conversation.

When Mama told Ray and Clay about the Granny incident, they had not seemed particularly upset. Clay had shaken his head and said he was going to Bobby's, and Ray had shrugged. I noticed, however, that neither one of them seemed keen on going into Granny's room. That made sense; the room was already pretty creepy. There was the dresser for one thing, in the bottom drawer of which I had once found Granny's hair.

My original impression—that somebody had been scalped—was wide of the mark. Granny had suffered a fever back around 1901, and the finest medical minds in Pike County, Alabama, had concluded that best practices required she cut off her hair. Granny, probably muttering, had complied but had felt unable to part with her tresses, which were a pretty light brown. I wasn't sure what we were supposed to do with them. The closet was another scary feature. Other than Granny's clothing, it contained large frightening portraits of Granny's parents, who had once had some money. Judging from their grim expressions, they must have had a premonition that they were shortly to lose everything.

I stayed out of Granny's room, but I wasn't sure what other precautions you were supposed to take if you were living in a haunted house, though moving seemed to be an option. To make matters worse, I had made the mistake of reading a book entitled *The Haunting of Hill House*, which I should have known to avoid. This book involved a group of morons who let themselves be talked into spending the night in a haunted house, with predictable results. By the final chapter, whatever was haunting the house had startled one of the morons into running her car into a nearby tree, after which she also had to haunt Hill House.

I shouldn't have read *Dracula* either, although I was nearly positive that Granny wasn't a vampire.

Meanwhile, although I could stay out of Granny's room, avoiding it altogether wasn't possible. My room was upstairs and on the way up I had to pass right in front of Granny's door. I didn't hear anything else, but was bothered by the sensation that something wanted me to look in the room.

To avoid accidentally doing this, I would shield my eyes with my hand while climbing the stairs, a move which put me in immediate peril of slipping and landing on the floor furnace.

At night the situation got worse. To go to the bathroom, I had to navigate the length of the house, passing the door of the former attic.

Although Granny was unlikely to be in the attic, I was very hesitant about passing the door. At least it was dark, so I didn't have to shut my eyes to avoid seeing anything.

I decided to confide in Annette. I figured she was prepared to accept my story since although she had just turned sixteen, she still slept with a night light. Annette had listened concernedly but when asked whether the Catholic Church could help with the situation said she thought you had to be a Catholic. She also seemed pretty hesitant the next time I invited her over.

Mama and I considered Ella's advice. Where were we going to get a horseshoe? I had already had enough trouble once when I became concerned that Dracula might be out in the backyard. We didn't have garlic, and I wasn't sure if garlic powder was the same thing.

My real worry was that Granny, or whoever was hanging around her room, would influence me to resume walking in my sleep. I had had trouble with sleepwalking when I was little, occasionally waking up at the back door. Since I was currently sleeping up a steep flight of stairs at the bottom of which was a furnace, I was obviously not in the ideal situation as far as roaming around with my eyes shut was concerned. I finally put the wastebasket in front of the stairs, figuring that it would slow me down.

As the weeks passed, so did my fear of sleepwalking and I finally reached a conclusion which reassured me to a certain extent. If Granny was trying to haunt anybody, it would probably be Mama, with whom she had had the sort of relationship one normally sees between a cobra and a mongoose. Mama, whatever her actual experience had been, was still insisting that she didn't believe in ghosts.

Granny probably wasn't intending to haunt me; I was just what the news was always referring to as collateral damage.

Besides, if we asked around, we were almost bound to find somebody with a horseshoe.

Meanwhile, there was Granny's room, just sitting there empty, but when Mama asked Ray and Clay whether one of them would like to move in there, they both said, in unison, "No."

Boyfriends

I was a threat to try stealing people's boyfriends. The tendency went way back. In kindergarten, I had finagled a kid named Johnny away from a kid named Betsy by falsely claiming that I loved orange juice. I had developed this stratagem after noting that Johnny was the class' number one consumer of citrus-based drinks.

The fact that this was the only time I had been successful in poaching somebody's boyfriend didn't faze me.

I couldn't have been said to be motivated by envy (or not exclusively anyway) since as high school kicked off I actually had a sort of boyfriend.

He didn't count, though.

I had been introduced to Richie Pitts via his sister Cissy whom I knew vaguely from our beach trips when I was a kid. Our first date was to the State Fair, and although Richie bought me a corn dog, when he asked me to go steady my response in its entirety was "no."

I didn't intend to tie myself down, especially to somebody who, I noticed, was already showing signs of being a turkey. Besides, as it turned out we just weren't very much alike. For example, when he attempted to take me to task for swearing, I told him to go to hell.

"The grass is always greener," said Mama, who in her youth had stolen boyfriends left and right.

The only people whose boyfriends I had no interest in stealing were Patty Harris and Annette DeSalvo. Patty's boyfriend went to Catholic High with her, but ironically he was an Anglican who was fond of doing things like wearing orange socks for St. Patrick's Day. He also had a part-time job selling Avon. To top things off, his name was Leslie which, I had informed Patty on more than one occasion, was a girl's name. She insisted on calling him Les, which wasn't fooling anybody.

Meanwhile, Annette had scored a coup by dating a boy in actual college. The trouble was, he was a jerk. His name was Henry but he insisted on being called Hal. When the movie *2001* came out we all started calling him Hal 9000 after the evil computer, but when I first met him the movie didn't exist so I had to improvise; whenever Annette wasn't around I just referred to Hal as "that jerk." Hal was a Catholic, which may have been the main attraction outside of his status as a college student, but he made up for his good qualities by being insanely jealous.

Since he was away at school pretty much all the time, you would think Annette had a relatively clear field, but unfortunately Hal had a big family and there was always somebody available to spy on Annette if she went out with, or even talked to, anybody else. On one occasion when I went to Panama City Beach with Annette and her parents, Hal had caused a sensation by suddenly appearing, having followed us all the way from Montgomery. He had treated me and Annette to dinner and seemed favorably disposed toward me, probably figuring that with me and her parents along Annette had had no opportunity to stray. In fact, that very afternoon she had met somebody at the Miracle Strip Amusement Park and had ridden the Octopus with him. I knew better than to say anything.

Meanwhile, I was now in the market for a boyfriend. Richie and I had parted ways before Christmas following a debacle in which he had telephoned to invite me to a Christmas formal, then telephoned five minutes later to uninvite me, saying that I would have to wear a fancy dress and it wouldn't be worth it. I yielded to no one in the fanciness of my dresses, most of which I had made, and I knew a phony excuse when I heard one. I figured that the little jerk had neglected to check with his father, a drunk Air Force doctor, before inviting me and that his father had declined to offer us a ride.

About this time, I targeted my cousin Sid as my future boyfriend. He had a regular girlfriend named Pam, but I figured I could beat her time because I sat next to Sid in English, giving me an opportunity to engage him in frivolous conversation whenever the teacher wasn't looking. To improve my odds, I decided to get contacts. This turned out to be easier said than done. The first contacts I got were ill-fitting; my eyes made an ominous clicking sound whenever I blinked. Finally, I got soft contact lenses which just sat there quietly so I felt confident in moving on to step two of my self-improvement plan, which was to do something about my hair.

I dyed it orange. This wasn't entirely on purpose.

The current hairstyle for girls was long, straight, and parted down the middle. You got extra points for being blonde. My hair was brown.

I could do the parted down the middle stuff, but my hair stopped growing about the time it reached my shoulders. Mama counseled me to put hot oil on it.

This didn't work.

Finally I decided that I should make my hair more interesting by doing something about the color. A product called Streaks N Tips became available about that time. The application procedure involved multiple steps. You pulled strands of your hair through a plastic cap, smeared on Streaks N Tips, waited a while, rinsed the product off, removed the cap and were left with brown hair interestingly streaked and/or tipped with blonde. One day while I was waiting, I got what seemed like a foolproof idea. I was friends with a girl named Janine whose hair was an interesting caramel color. I reasoned that all I had to do was remove the cap, comb Streaks N Tips entirely through my hair and immediately wash it. The result would be interesting caramel-colored hair made even more interesting by the blonde streaks and tips.

Instead, my hair turned orange.

Had this occurred on Halloween, Mama would probably not have been as upset.

As it was, she put in an emergency call to the Montgomery Fair beauty shop, where she knew people, and I was hauled off there to have my hair dyed completely, and boringly, brown.

I finally abandoned my pursuit of Sid when he gave Pam a star sapphire ring which would have looked swell on me, but by this time I had set my sights on somebody else.

Lizzie Holt, whose record with boyfriends was even more dismal than mine, had introduced me to her friend Francie, whose father was in the Air Force. Francie had in turn introduced me to her brother Thor. Thor was not, unfortunately, the blond Viking type. He had been named, God knows why, for a friend of his father's from World War Two. Thor was an improvement over Richie partly because of his family's house which was in the modern Normandale subdivision and had central heat and air. Besides that, he had lived in Japan and his mother knew how to make sukiyaki.

That was pretty much it.

Nevertheless, I was hanging around with Thor when I noticed that Francie's boyfriend, Tom, was much more my type. He knew a lot better jokes than Thor, who tended to want to discuss his rock collection. Also, Tom had a car.

It was no trouble at all to inveigle Francie into suggesting that Thor and I double date with her and Tom. Thor was pretty annoyed that I kept leaning over the seat to talk to Tom, but Francie didn't even seem to notice. She was going through an odd phase. She said "wow" a lot, was a threat to just sit there staring off into space, and sometimes she went to sleep while talking to you. I wasn't sure what was going on, but figured her unusual behavior would give a boost to my plan to swipe Tom, since he would be bound to notice how wide-awake I was.

It was Thor who came up with the idea of going to visit the Glowing Grave. This phenomenon was located in an old abandoned cemetery off the Mobile Road. Many people had reported seeing an eerily-glowing tombstone in the graveyard, and some people had heard things. I regarded the Glowing Grave as a vital part of my plan, which involved showing intrepidity in the face of the spectral tombstone. No matter how bright it got, I wasn't going to act scared. Meanwhile, Francie, if she even noticed the grave, was bound to say something senseless, like "wow," and Thor, I figured, would probably run off. Tom was certain to react with even more bravery than I planned on displaying, and would suddenly realize that he and I were kindred spirits, so to speak.

At first, the plan worked pretty well. On the way to the graveyard, leaning over the seat, I engaged Tom in witty conversation, while Thor fumed and Francie, yawning, asked if anybody had any potato chips. The graveyard turned out to be extremely dark and overgrown. We all got out of the car and stumbled around, occasionally falling over a tombstone. Suddenly, Thor gasped. "There it is!" He pointed unsteadily at a tombstone which was, in fact, sort of glowing. Then the glow faded, only to start up again a few seconds later. I peered at the tombstone. The glow was, I realized, just the gleam of headlights from cars turning off the Mobile Road hitting a headstone made of unusually shiny granite.

"Run!" yelled Tom.

"But it's just headlights," I tried to say, only to be drowned out by Thor yelling "Back in the car!" and Francie yelling "Wow!"

We all piled into the car and bounced away. This was disappointing. Tom was as big a chicken as Thor.

I sighed. Back to the drawing board.

1968

The year 1968 got off to a bad start. Then, things went downhill.

Granny died not long after the first of the year. Though she was dead, she was in no apparent hurry to vacate the premises, so we all lay awake at night, thinking we heard things.

One of the things we heard was Ray, up and down all night drinking water, then up a short while later to visit the bathroom. It finally got to the point that Mama took him to the doctor.

I was sitting in my upstairs sanctuary when Mama's head appeared over the top of the stairwell.

"Ray's got diabetes," she said. In fact, he had juvenile onset diabetes—the kind where you have to have a shot every day.

This was a low blow. Of all the family, Ray was on record as hating shots the most. When we were little and had to be dragged to the hospital once a year to have polio shots, Ray always fought the most tenaciously, once announcing that he'd rather have polio. Ray's illness had the unintentional effect of ending my tentative career plans. I was thinking of being a nurse, since I was devoted to *Star Trek* and *Star Trek* had nurses. I figured when the United States finally allowed women to be astronauts, if I was already a nurse I'd have an inside track. When we all went to the doctor's office to see them demonstrate correct shot technique, I watched interestedly until the nurse plunged the demonstration needle into a wadded-up pillow. The pillow made a popping sound. I fainted.

Spring rolled in. Ray, complaining bitterly, shot himself every morning. I abandoned my plans of being a nurse along with my efforts to learn how to make pecan pie; Ray couldn't have sugar. Mama got a copy of *The Diabetics' Cookbook* and I practiced making banana bread with saccharine, which tasted about like it sounds.

I had always depended on television to distract me from what was going on in my daily life; this tendency went all the way back to *Captain Kangaroo*. Getting distracted was more difficult now that the airwaves had been pretty much taken over by the real world. For example, every night the news featured a running total of how many people had been killed in Viet Nam.

Then came a television announcement that sounded like good news: President Johnson wouldn't run for reelection. This was a relief. By this time half the country hated Johnson for Viet Nam and the other half hated him for the Civil Rights Act, while everybody hated him for picking up his dogs by the ears. Whoever we got next time couldn't possibly be as bad.

Contentment reigned for four days, after which Martin Luther King went to Memphis.

There followed a period when all the news programs showed cities on fire. Every night, you'd turn on the television and there would be Chicago, or Washington, or Detroit, or Baltimore burning down, with a caption to tell you which one it was today. At school, the situation was a little less volatile; there still weren't many black students at Lanier, though the general feeling was that they might be up to something. This may have been why the shop students decided to go on a war footing. They all started spending their class time making weapons, the most popular of which was a section of broom handle, hollowed out and filled with molten metal. After all that effort, there was no real trouble at school, barring a sort of low-key simmering resentment. The shop students, frustrated, went back to learning how to replace a muffler.

During this period, Miss Bonnie, who could be counted on to announce that all hell was going to break loose at any moment, remained uncharacteristically silent. I kept waiting for her to advise us to stock up with bullets, but she never did. Mama said she was preoccupied with worrying about Lurleen.

Miss Bonnie was a secretary for the state legislature, but when Lurleen Wallace was elected governor because George Wallace couldn't succeed himself, Lurleen had hired Miss Bonnie as her personal secretary. At first, this was a glamorous job and Miss Bonnie could be counted on to regale Mama with tales of how she had helped Lurleen select the dress for her official portrait or what was being served for dinner at the Governor's Mansion. Now Lurleen had cancer. Every time Miss Bonnie came over, we got a bulletin about her prognosis. As spring wore on, the bulletins got shorter and grimmer. Somebody at school had read an article called "Lurleen Wallace Stricken with Cancer" which said that if she didn't die from the cancer, Lurleen would die from the radiation treatments.

She died from the cancer, and we went with Miss Bonnie to her funeral a couple of weeks before my birthday. The floral arrangements stretched all the way up the cemetery drive nearly to our family's plot.

In the midst of all this we got a breather when the movie *2001* came out. The big deal with this movie, besides the evil computer, was the "light show" scene where the spaceship is careening through space. Apparently the correct procedure was to watch the light show while stoned. My cousin Sid, whom I still sat next to in English, decided that it would be more practical to get drunk. It didn't work the same way, he'd reported sadly. All he did was throw up.

Planet of the Apes hit town about the same time. At the end of the movie, you find out that it's been taking place on Earth the whole time and that monkeys are now in charge. Really, this was as bad as the news. Besides, neither movie could exactly be called escapist entertainment since first you had to sit through a newsreel about Viet Nam which always showed soldiers slogging through mud.

Finally, school was out for the summer. We headed to Gulf Shores, where we had spent happy times when I was little. The cottages we used to stay in were long since torn down, so we were in a motel called the Rolling Tide which was distinguished by the fact that you parked under the building, and by the fact that the floors creaked. It was possible to hear the surf if you opened the door, however, and we were enjoying a peaceful evening when somebody turned on the television.

Robert Kennedy had been shot.

"Turn it off," I said.

I was sorry that I didn't have television as a reliable distraction that summer, because I had time on my hands. I didn't have a summer job. I was concentrating on learning how to cook from *The Diabetics' Cookbook* and making some clothes to wear in the fall.

Meanwhile, the nightly news got steadily worse. A lot more people were getting drafted and sent to Viet Nam. My friend Janine's older brother went for his draft physical and came back too shaken to discuss what they'd done to him. Around this time, the news stopped showing rioting related to Martin Luther King's assassination and started showing rioting relating to Viet Nam.

Some of the worst rioting was taking place at the Democratic Convention in Chicago. It was featured every night on the news since the riot police had waded into the antiwar demonstrators right in front of the cameras. Shortly after the convention finished, the news reported that in addition to hippies, we now had Yippies, who were sort of political hippies. "Great," I thought sourly. I wasn't even used to the hippies yet. As far as anyone could figure out, the Yippies were opposed to Viet Nam and pay toilets, so they had something for everybody.

School started and Clay was back in Cloverdale, having spent the summer begging Mama not to make him go back to Williams. He seemed happier if no more talkative and his hair soon grew back out. Meanwhile, Mama had decided to move the television into Granny's old room since nobody was willing to sleep there, so the living room stayed cleaner.

Big news now was the election. Nixon was running against Humphrey and Wallace, who had a particularly scary commercial. It showed a woman walking down a dark street, her high heels clicking. Then it showed a streetlight. Then somebody shot out the streetlight. Then the woman's footsteps stopped.

When Election Day finally arrived, Nixon won on a platform of Law and Order which probably appealed to anybody who had watched the news even once that year. It was a foregone conclusion, as Mama had said, that Alabama would go for Wallace. Humphrey had run on a platform of continuing what Johnson had started; I was surprised he hadn't run on a platform of ending the war. I confided to Miss Bonnie that I thought he would have stood a better chance if he had. Miss Bonnie, who had recovered somewhat from Lurleen's death and was back to being a secretary for the legislature, disagreed with me. She said that if Viet Nam went Communist we would have the domino effect with the result that Australia would go Communist. I agreed that this would be bad.

Then at the last minute, the television situation improved. On Christmas Eve, the Apollo Eight spaceship orbited the moon and we all got to see its other side for the first time. It had, frankly, a lot more craters than the front side. The astronauts read from Genesis as they orbited.

I didn't exactly feel merry, but I felt more relaxed than I had in months. There wasn't going to be any peace on earth, but if we could all stay alive another week, 1968 would be history.

Hair

The first time I heard about the musical *Hair* I was in English class. Lizzie, who sat behind me, had passed me a magazine with a cover photo of a lot of people with hair. People did pass things in class; one time in algebra somebody had handed me a copy of *The Group* with all the naughty stuff underlined.

This was different, though. This was Miss Molston's class. Miss Molston was a crazy old hag who reminded me so much of my teachers at Cloverdale that I wondered why on earth she wasn't teaching there. Maybe teaching at Lanier was considered a promotion since it would enable her to torment a larger audience. Miss Molston concentrated on making us hate the English language by forcing us to diagram sentences on the board and by criticizing us if the chalk dust made us sneeze.

Since I was afraid of Miss Molston, I stowed the magazine in my history book to be reviewed later. As soon as I dug it out, I could tell that *Hair* was a controversial play. For one thing, it was supposed to be about hippies, but these were militant antiwar hippies who, when not hopping around the stage naked, hopped around the stage acting like they were totally wasted. There was a possibility that they weren't acting. Up until then, the only hippies I was familiar with were the ones on television during coverage of life in the Haight-Ashbury district of San Francisco. Those hippies didn't seem interested in the war; they were depicted as spending most of their time smiling, staring into space, going "wow," and handing people flowers.

The program had featured a hippie couple getting married during a Be-in in a park. Another hippie was officiating; he pronounced the happy couple married "so long as you both shall dig it," after which everybody dropped acid and somebody played a tape of the songs of the humpback whale. Patty Harris had been profoundly interested in the hippie scene and had announced that she was running away to San Francisco to get away from her mother, Clara, who was officially crazy. I had urged Patty to go, since I figured that was a good chance to get rid of her, but she had re-thought when Clara announced that she would buy Patty a Volkswagen when she learned to drive.

After the *Hair* magazine came out, I kept my eyes peeled for signs of hippies, but I never really saw any. *Hair*, on the other hand, resurfaced pretty often. First the radio started playing selections from the soundtrack. The main song started out "Gimme a head with HAIR! Long, beautiful HAIR!!!!" and went on catchily in that vein. I had a feeling the album might contain some good songs, but I didn't want to spend money on it. Patty Harris usually had soundtrack albums from Broadway plays lying around since Clara thought they were cultural, but I didn't think she would find *Hair* cultural compared to, say, *Oklahoma*.

The next time *Hair* showed up was, weirdly, during halftime of the Lee-Lanier game. This football game was a major event, since Robert E. Lee High School was Lanier's crosstown rival and had been founded in the 1950s to siphon off all the rednecks. This was similar to the way Jeff Davis had recently been founded to allow rich kids and hangers-on like Patty Harris to escape going to school with normal people. The Lee-Lanier game was played at Cramton Bowl, the big football stadium downtown, and since there was always a chance of violence everybody went. I had been wandering around at halftime looking for the bathroom and was headed back to my seat when I heard a familiar tune coming from the field. It was "Aquarius" from *Hair* and it was being played full blast by the Lanier band. I didn't think the band was exactly pro-hippie and at any event the next selection they played was the theme from *Hawaii Five-0* but obviously *Hair* had made somewhat of an inroad.

Long hair, in addition to inspiring the popular musical, was increasingly in evidence in school. Ray and Clay both sported luxuriant growth, though since they were still in junior high it wasn't considered threatening enough to be strictly regulated. At Lanier, there was some effort to restrain the guys but the administration was still more interested in blighting the lives of the more fashion-conscious girls. Besides, a lot of the kids at Lanier were from military families, since Montgomery had two Air Force bases. Guys from these families weren't encouraged to grow their hair to its fullest potential and a lot of them were, in fact, in ROTC. These guys were probably headed to Viet Nam, but not right away. The ones going to college would get deferments and by the time they graduated maybe everything would be over.

The big event of the year for ROTC was the visit by a commanding officer from one of the air bases. He would review the cadets on the football field, after which there would be a military ball in the gym. There had been some random muttering earlier in the year to the effect that the military should not have a presence at school, much less be throwing formal dances in our gym, but everybody sort of ignored it. This kind of controversy was a symptom of the time, though. Early in the year there had been what was usually reported as an "uprising" at Columbia University in New York, which involved students taking over the administration building, holding a faculty member hostage and, according to one report, sticking a poster of Lenin up on the wall, and this uprising had been prompted partly by the college's ties to the military.

I didn't think anybody at Lanier was going to take a teacher hostage and if they did I hoped it would be Miss Molston, since that would serve everybody right, but as it turned out Lanier's subversive element had had other plans. Somebody got hold of the football field line marker and by the time the Air Force general arrived, the word PAX had been spelled out on the football field in chalk letters twenty feet long. They apparently didn't have enough chalk to spell PEACE.

On that happy note, classes were dismissed for the holidays.

I had spent a peaceful Christmas Eve watching the astronauts orbit the moon and was still in a good mood the next day as I opened my presents, including a cache of albums and a formal with a satin skirt and velveteen top which, frankly, I didn't see myself getting to wear any time soon. Patty Harris had survived her usual holiday experience of having Clara chase her around the house with a butcher knife for being ungrateful. When the incident was reported to me, I staunchly repeated my advice to Patty that she should head straight for the Haight, but Patty replied that she was waiting until she got the Volkswagen so she could drive there.

That afternoon I got an excited call from Lizzie. "Guess what? I got the *Hair* album!"

She was more excited about this than I would have been, but I agreed that we should get together and listen to it before school started back.

In fact, we listened to it New Year's Eve. Lizzie's parents were going to a party at the Officers Club and Lizzie was on tap to babysit Jane, her younger sister, who was guaranteed to spend the evening announcing that she didn't need a babysitter. I had been happy to accept the invitation, Jane or no Jane, because I loved visiting Lizzie's house, which was located in a scenic wooded area and which had central heat and air. We were happily singing "Long as I can grow it my HAIR!!!" when Ann, Lizzie's older sister, emerged gloomily from her room to tell us to shut up.

"She's depressed," whispered Lizzie after Ann had gone back in the room, which was painted black including the ceiling and would depress anybody. I had met Ann nearly two years earlier. She had distinguished herself by taking part in an anti-war protest in Washington, D.C., where she had been in college. After she got arrested, Mr. Holt had bailed her out on condition that she transfer to Auburn University, which was not a hotbed of revolt. Although she was home for the holidays, Ann was having a blue Christmas because she was enamored of one of her fellow protesters, a guy named Frank who was still in Washington but who, according to Lizzie, was thinking seriously of heading for Canada.

Following Ann's appearance, we watched Dick Clark for awhile with Jane, then when it became 1969 in New York, we went outside and walked down the road. The stars were brilliant; so was the moon, from which the astronauts had by this time returned.

"Let the sunshine in," we sang. 1968 was over. Whatever was coming couldn't get any worse.

"Happy New Year," I said.

Land of a Thousand Dances

I had mixed luck with dances. I had attended one back when I was still in Cloverdale but it was a complete bust since nobody asked to dance with me. It's possible I shouldn't have worn a sack dress. The loafers probably didn't help either. Bobby Dobbs' mother tried to cheer me up by pointing out that nobody asked her daughter Brenda to dance the first time either. This wasn't much comfort, since Brenda Dobbs, despite being older than me and a fount of information on topics ranging from wolverines to the hydrogen bomb, had turned out to be a poor judge of human nature. At 16, she eloped with Holk Collins, a kid from a rich family. So far so good, yet just a few weeks later he had tried to kill Brenda by locking her in a room into which he had lobbed a roach bomb. Brenda, reeking of insecticide, had crawled out a window and Mama had helped her get an annulment, but I still didn't consider her a role model.

Things went slightly better at a church dance I attended with Patty Harris. I got fed up with waiting around and asked a guy to dance to "Satisfaction," while Patty moaned that nobody was asking her to dance because she looked too young. I could have told her the pigtails were a mistake.

I had assumed that dances in high school would be more entertaining but the first dance I attended at Lanier wasn't much, even though I technically had a date with Richie Pitts, whose older sister Cissy currently fancied herself a hippie. A big horsey-looking girl, she said "wow" a lot and occasionally showed up with an artificial daisy in her hair.

The Lanier freshman dance had been a huge affair; herds of kids roaming around the gym, groups sitting on bleachers and, if anybody was fool enough to try dancing, a crowd of onlookers surrounding them as if they were at a dogfight. Nevertheless I danced with Richie a couple of times while scanning the room for somebody better. Cissy then appalled me by asking Richie to dance. I was already pretty much appalled because, even though she was supposed to be a hippie, she had shown up in knee socks. Dancing with her brother was, I thought, probably illegal but I wasn't sure what I could do about it.

Luckily, Lanier wasn't the only school in town. When Annette asked if I wanted to go to a dance at Catholic High, I was a little surprised that she wasn't going with Hal, who was home from college for a change. It turned out that Hal's family had decamped to visit relatives in Huntsville, and Annette didn't want to show up alone. The dance at Catholic was an improvement. They had refreshments and you didn't have to sit on bleachers. Also there were fewer people, which turned out to be a good thing. There were only 31 people in Annette's class, so anybody new tended to attract attention, and I danced every dance and got invited to their prom by a guy who, it turned out, I never heard from again. I had a better time than Annette, since nobody asked her to dance out of fear it would get back to Hal, who was known for his temper.

Mama was naturally upset that I wasn't being the belle of the ball at anyplace which did not involve Catholics. She had been a hit at dances back in the Depression and had dated an entire CCC camp. She gave me several wardrobe hints but finally decided that the problem must be that I didn't know how to dance. "I was the same way," she sighed. "I had two left feet." In fact, she still had her old Arthur Murray charts with little footprints to indicate how you were supposed to do the Fox Trot or whatever, but obviously the guys who were mobbing her at dances hadn't cared.

Besides that, dancing had either evolved or atrophied since Mama was young. I had mastered the Twist in sixth grade, but after that the options had exploded. Now you had a choice. You could spend all your free time practicing the Cool Jerk, the Pony, the Mashed Potato, and the Swim, or you could just get out there and writhe.

Time marched on. I brightened up the occasional Catholic High dance and once was invited to their 25 cent Spaghetti Supper by a guy who, said Annette censoriously, had a regular girlfriend out of town. Mama got used to greeting me after a dance with "Well? Did you have a good time?" and being answered with a noncommittal shrug.

Then help arrived from an unexpected quarter. Francie invited me to go with her and Lizzie to a Civil Air Patrol dance. Civil Air Patrol was an organization which was on call to search for wrecked planes. Since there usually weren't any wrecked planes, the members spent most of their free time having meetings and going to dances. I wondered why Francie wasn't going with Tom, but it turned out the couple were on the rocks and Francie figured she would make him jealous by being a hit at a dance.

CAP held its dances on the air base, a huge, confusing place at which, it was rumored, it was possible to buy gas for 25 cents a gallon. The dance itself was in a big ramshackle building which must have served a multitude of purposes since it included a full kitchen and movie screen. I was impressed, both by the movie screen and by the fact that around 80% of the CAP consisted of guys. This, I felt, was actually more like it. Besides, they had a lot of Rolling Stones records.

I was happily dancing away when I sensed controversy developing. The dances at Lanier were nominally integrated, but since the respective races weren't even interested in dancing with their own members they were hardly likely to dance with each other. The CAP dances were actually integrated, and the setting had evidently inspired Francie to hurl herself at Darius Barganier, who was on the Student Council and whose jealous girlfriend, Jamelle, was standing right there. I suddenly felt I needed a Coke so I wandered into the room I had earlier identified as the kitchen, only to discover that it was a storeroom and that there were a lot of people in there grabbing armloads of toilet paper. I wondered if it was a sort of black market heist, since on the base toilet paper was probably even cheaper than gas.

"Shut that door," barked a guy who had apparently appointed himself the leader.

"What's going on?" I asked.

"Toilet papering a trailer," barked the guy again. "You in?"

"Sure," I said. This toilet papering looked premeditated. Many of the team had taken the precaution of wearing black, and I was fairly visible in a red dress which Mama had made me shorten, but I figured they knew what they were doing.

Fully loaded with toilet paper, we skulked off via the back door. The trailer turned out to belong to one of the dance chaperones, a burly woman I had seen prowling the sidelines emitting an occasional growl. This woman, Sergeant Cooley, did not have a big following despite her willingness to serve as chaperone; in fact, several members of the toilet paper committee were referring to her disrespectfully as Melvin Cooley, G-Man. She had the further misfortune of inhabiting a trailer within easy walking distance of the CAP dance.

My previous experience with toilet papering had involved conventional houses where the object was to lob the toilet paper into surrounding trees or, in a pinch, bushes. Toilet papering a trailer was slightly more complicated; the correct procedure was to wrap the entire trailer by rolling the paper underneath, then throwing it over the top. The gang I was with were obviously professionals; the trailer ended up looking like a mummy.

Finally the head toilet paper guy gave the result a satisfied look, appearing to think that his work here was done, and everybody dispersed, sneaking back into the dance and, in my case, getting a badly-needed Coke. Darius was back to dancing with his girlfriend. I didn't see Francie but Lizzie, who was eating a donut, reported that she was hiding in the bathroom.

When I got home, Mama said "Well? How was your dance?" and I said "Great."

Daylight Robbery

We had to dress out for gym. Then we had to do something with our stuff. The gym didn't have lockers; it had wire baskets with no locks on them, and that's where the trouble started.

Lanier, which looked like a fortress, was largely undefended. Anybody could waltz in with perfect ease; the administration probably figured who would want to?

One winter day, I grudgingly donned my blue one-piece gym outfit, which could have passed for bloomers had the pants been a little longer, and stuffed my real clothes and purse into the basket.

My finances had improved; in fact, I had just received $10 as a reward for a sterling report card.

I had carefully put the $10 away in my wallet's secret compartment, figuring that it was safe from prying eyes.

As it turned out I was wrong.

I was in the middle of dodgeball, at which I excelled since by constant practice I had developed the ability to hide behind even the smallest girl, when the whistle blew. I was somewhat relieved; I had been convinced that the last ball had had my name on it. Mrs. Harrison looked grave. We had, she announced, been robbed.

Sure enough, when we got to the changing room, my wallet was lying on the floor, the secret compartment gaping open. Two other girls—Sherry James and Janet McCoy—had also suffered depredations.

There was good news, though; the robber was already in custody. This robber turned out to be a black teenager who had waltzed in, made a beeline for the wire baskets, and was preparing to waltz back out with her ill-gotten gains when she ran into trouble in the shape of Mary Porter, who was white, and Deloris Jackson, who was black. Even then she might have avoided detection; in a school of 1600 students, not everybody knew everybody else. However, she was pregnant.

At Lanier, pregnancy was invisible. Even in cases where it was common knowledge that the wedding had been an unwelcome surprise to all parties, as soon as the expectant mother started to become obvious about it, she was out of there. Deloris and Mary knew an impostor when they saw one. They summoned help, the police were called, and the robber was already on her way downtown by the time we were notified.

Meanwhile, where was my $10? It developed that my report card money was in the evidence room at the police station, at which everybody connected with the robbery was required to show up.

Unlike Lanier, the police station really was a fortress. We were herded through the grim building into a room with a window. Mary and Deloris, having caught the robber red-handed, would be viewing a lineup.

I was interested. Had the cops gone out and dragooned a selection of pregnant black teenagers? If they hadn't found enough pregnant ones would they require the decoys to stuff pillows down their dresses?

Unfortunately, I didn't get to find out. I had to go to the bathroom. This was always happening.

Muttering, I excused myself and went looking for a bathroom. The police station was like a maze; I was a little lost heading back to the lineup, and that is when I ran into the bum.

Why was a bum in a police station? It didn't make any sense. All I knew was that this scary bum appeared, accosted me and said something which sounded a lot like "Xxbn cyrrrwm?"

"No sir," I said, figuring that would cover all the bases. Then I fled.

The lineup was, of course, over by the time I got back.

Next we had to show up for the grand jury. Sherry, Janet, and I probably wouldn't have to do anything, we were told. Instead, we were supposed to wait in the courthouse hall while Deloris and Mary once again testified. Deloris came out; Mary went in. This hallway didn't have chairs. The only thing to sit on was the air conditioner unit which was not on since it was January. Sherry, Janet, and I plopped ourselves on it and Sherry announced happily that her mother had had a great idea; a spend-the-night party for the robbery contingent. Then she noticed Deloris and stopped talking. I thought a distraction was called for, so I got off the air conditioner. "You want to sit down?" I asked Deloris. Deloris shook her head. I felt sort of bad so I didn't sit down either.

At this point Mary re-emerged, looking embarrassed. She had been testifying away and had reached the part where she saw the robber. "I knew she wasn't a student," she said. When asked how she knew, Mary was supposed to say "because she was pregnant," but she was too embarrassed to say "pregnant" so she blurted out "there was something wrong with her stomach."

The grand jury had started laughing and Mary was dismissed.

That was it except for the hearing, for which we also had to show up and for which I had to get out of English class. Miss Molston was a vicious old bat but I figured she knew better than to mess with somebody who was helping the police.

"I won't be in class Thursday," I announced matter-of-factly. Molston gave me an evil stare.

"I have to appear in court."

Molston didn't disappoint. Throwing her hands in the air, she whinnied, "Oh my Lordy goodness gracious me!" She didn't say "Lawsy mercy!" but she was clearly thinking it, so I went and sat down.

The hearing was pretty anti-climactic. We all sat in the audience section of the courtroom. The robber appeared to be wearing her own clothes rather than a jail uniform, perhaps because they didn't have maternity uniforms. She was asked how she pleaded.

"Guilty," she said, speaking right up. Maybe she'd been there before.

That was it. Nobody had to testify.

Lizzie, when I reported to her, said I should show some compassion for the poor pregnant girl, who might have been driven to steal by desperation. I said I could certainly understand how Lizzie might feel that way, and meanwhile where was my damn $10?

The only thing left was the spend-the-night party.

Everybody except Deloris assembled at the James house in Normandale. Mrs. James, a big fat woman, bustled around beaming and fixing hamburgers. "It's so nice to meet some of Sherry's little friends," she said. Sherry rolled her eyes. It was cold and overcast outside, so after dinner we just sat around talking and playing Sherry's Beach Boys albums."I shouldn't have talked about the party in front of her," said Sherry, referring to Deloris, "but you know I just couldn't have her showing up here."

"She wouldn't expect to be invited," said Janet reassuringly.

I knew Deloris wouldn't expect to be invited, and that if she had been accidentally invited, she wouldn't have come. In fact, I was wondering what I was doing there. I didn't know any of the other girls; I guessed we were just supposed to be united by misfortune. It struck me that being robbed was really a lousy excuse for a party.

Eventually *Star Trek* came on and I perked up a little. It was an odd episode, though; some aliens who wanted to hijack the starship Enterprise had turned 90% of the crew into little cubes and were threatening to squash them unless Captain Kirk cooperated. Captain Kirk foiled the aliens and got nearly everybody uncubed by the end, but really it was a pretty lackluster effort. I felt uneasy. *Star Trek* had been a major prop of my existence, but now it showed signs of sucking wind. What would I do if it was canceled?

"Hey!" somebody yelled about this time. "It's snowing!"

It really was snowing. Everybody ran outside to watch the little flakes spiraling under the streetlamp. Then Sherry's older sister Alice showed up. She appeared somewhat the worse for wear, rolling out of a car which then took off.

"She's drunk!" said Sherry gleefully.

"Am not!" said Alice, stumbling toward the house in a dignified manner. We all followed her in to see what Mrs. James would do but she had already gone to bed. Alice wandered into the room she shared with Sherry with everybody else piling in after her.

"You're totally wasted," said Sherry, warming to her theme. "Am nah," said Alice, collapsing on the bed.

"Oh yeah? Say 'aluminum.'"

Alice sat unsteadily up. She thought about it. "Aluminimum," she stated, before passing out.

That was pretty much it. The next morning, we found that none of the snow had stuck. We had biscuits with blackberry jam for breakfast, Mama arrived, and I left.

When I got in the car, Mama said "Jimmy says you need to go to the police station and make them give you your money back. Otherwise they're liable to keep it." Jimmy Cates was one of the lawyers Mama worked for and he was wise to the cops.

I was sufficiently alarmed to insist we head right to the police station. I figured they'd be open even though it was Saturday. Sure enough, they were open and doing a brisk business. I marched up to the evidence room window, introduced myself and said that my lawyer,

Jimmy Cates, had sent me to get my $10 back. The cop seemed a little nonplussed—he may have had plans for the money—but went away and came back with an envelope which proved to contain $10. I had no idea whether it was my original money.

A couple of weeks later Mama asked if I had seen Janet, Mary, or Sherry. "No," I said, though I had seen them as well as Deloris in the bathroom. Mama seemed disappointed. "Well, I think Mrs. James had planned for you girls to have a regular round of parties."

"I think everybody's busy," I said.

The case was closed.

Of everybody involved, I was the only one who got my money back.

Wow, Man

By the time Montgomery got a head shop I realized that I might have been a little naive about the spread of the drug culture. Actually, by this time Montgomery had two head shops. The African Head Shop was in a black neighborhood near Oak Park and The Magic Mushroom was within easy walking distance of our house. The Magic Mushroom allegedly didn't sell dope, but it had a pretty complete selection of dope-related accessories. The one time I went in there with Ray and Clay, they both bought hash pipes. This worried me a little.

I had associated drugs with hippies, but although Montgomery still had a hippie shortage, drugs were now becoming more widespread. This actually explained a lot. For one thing, I was starting to figure out why Francie was always saying "wow."

Last summer, she had lost her job at Dairy Queen. It seems whenever somebody ordered a double soft-serve cone, Francie would become fascinated by watching the vanilla soft-serve spiral out of the machine. She would stand there gazing at the rapidly-building cone, occasionally saying "wow," until the cone got about a foot tall and fell over.

Her flirtation with drugs had apparently taken its toll on her relationship with Tom. Even though she had given him a fringed leather jacket for Christmas, he showed no signs of turning into a hippie. Finally, they had parted company.

This should have been good news for me, but it wasn't. For one thing, I had become disillusioned with Tom for behaving like a chicken in the face of the Glowing Grave. For another thing, he had started showing an interest in me. I had discovered a troubling, and possibly disastrous, trait in myself: I only liked people who didn't like me. Ideally, I liked people who didn't realize I existed. If somebody started liking me, that sort of blew it.

Even overlooking the above objections, Tom was out of the running because he had announced he wasn't going to college. I was going to college. It had been decided way back, even though I disliked school enough to be a natural candidate for leaving at the age of sixteen. When I was a kid, my father had planned on me becoming a history teacher, pointing out that they could make upwards of $12,000 a year. After my father died, though, it became assumed that I would go to law school since I was the eldest and since Ray and Clay had even less interest in education than I had.

I thought my brothers were a little young to get involved with Montgomery's fledgling drug culture, but after they got the hash pipes I started wondering. Clay was undoubtedly relieved to be back in Cloverdale Junior High. The only class he liked was art, but he didn't have to wear a uniform, and his hair was back to its usual flamboyant length, so things were looking up for him. Ray was having a problem coping with his diabetes. He took his shots and checked his blood by sticking his finger (this prompted even more complaining from him than the shots) but he didn't stay on his diet despite all Mama's fussing over him.

He absolutely wasn't supposed to drink, so it came as an unwelcome surprise when he and his friend Larry Nix were discovered dead drunk on the lawn of the First Methodist Church. The incident was quickly hushed up, but it had an effect on Ray: he apparently decided that marijuana was a lot safer.

Meanwhile, drugs were becoming well-entrenched at Lanier, although the administration was pretending otherwise. Football games had acquired a mellow haze, though the team was still ferocious enough. The fact that they remained belligerent didn't mean they weren't smoking dope. As somebody pointed out, the Hell's Angels smoked dope, and look at them.

People were as usual smoking in the bathrooms, though the smell had altered. Then somebody planted marijuana in the library's potted ficus. Apparently people were watering it from the drinking fountain, with some difficulty since the old bat in charge of the library was not going to let you bring in any water. I'm not sure what she thought was going on with the ficus. Maybe she assumed home ec had something to do with the added plant. I saw this plant one time before somebody harvested it; by this time it had reached roughly five feet and was hard to miss.

As for Francie, she had gotten so weird that whenever I went anywhere with her and Lizzie, Lizzie drove. Matters finally reached the point where Francie's altered state nearly got me in trouble with the *North Tower*. This was the high school literary magazine and Lizzie, Francie and I were heavily involved. We had editorial meetings in which I usually wound up doing something like explaining why a student's poem about the Democratic Convention which rhymed "told them so," with "windy Chicago" was a lousy poem only to find that the poem had been submitted anonymously by the Assistant Editor's boyfriend, who had written it especially for her.

One early spring evening, Francie and I were headed to a meeting, Lizzie driving, when I mentioned that I was very proud of a poem I had submitted which had been inspired by a story in one of the science fiction books I was always reading, usually in algebra class. During the meeting, my poem—submitted anonymously—came up for consideration right after Refreshments, in the course of which Francie had eaten five donuts. I smiled confidently. At this point, Francie, prefacing her remarks with a censorious "wow," said that the poem was plagiarized from a science fiction book. Then she went to sleep.

Lizzie and I exchanged looks. The situation was salvaged by Eileen Hickam, who said so what if it was plagiarized, and anyway the fact that the poem had already been in a book was proof it was good. Everybody agreed. Francie didn't remember the incident later.

As the weather warmed up, Ray and Clay began spending most of their time away from home. In Clay's case this was routine, but it was unusual for them to hang around together. One day Ray left an old copy of *Rolling Stone* lying on the couch; it was pretty interesting and in fact had a lot of helpful advice for novice pot growers. I wondered if the library people had read it.

During this time Ray and Clay began playing a Jimi Hendrix album practically nonstop. One April day I went out in the backyard to escape from "All Along the Watchtower" and was idly surveying the forsythia bush when I noticed something odd on the carport roof. Mama had had the carport added to our one-car garage about the time we got a second car. Our 1958 Bel Air still occupied the garage, but the carport was now home to a 1965 Plymouth Mama had bought from a lawyer where she worked.

The carport roof, usually uninteresting, had sprouted a row of planters. This was unusual enough to prompt me to haul out the ladder. Sure enough, there were ten thriving pot plants, obviously well cared for. I was in something of a quandary. I didn't want to get busted for living on a pot plantation. On the other hand, if I hadn't told on Francie I didn't see where I would get off telling on my own family. Matters got considerably worse the following month, when on one rainy day I grabbed Mama's old raincoat and found a baggie full of pot in the pocket. Something's got to give, I thought, and sure enough, something did.

Abicat started coughing. He drooped around, not eating and obviously miserable. We were all scared. The previous year he had suffered from what the vet called pernicious anemia and we had been worried he would die; Mama had saved his life by feeding him nothing but hamburger meat for months.

When Mama and I dragged Abi to the doctor, packing him in an old picnic basket for the trip, the vet seemed puzzled. "Has he been exposed to marijuana?" "Oh, no," said Mama obliviously. I didn't say anything. "Because," said the vet, eyeing me severely if unjustly, "Many cats are violently allergic to marijuana pollen. It can cause a fatal reaction." He gave Abi a cortisone shot and we took him home, where Mama gave him some Gerber's baby food.

"I don't understand it," said Mama that evening to Ray and Clay, who were staring off into space as usual. "Dr. Blake thinks Abicat's been exposed to marijuana pollen. It could be fatal." "Wow," said Ray and Clay unhappily. Then they disappeared into their room and fired up "All Along the Watchtower."

I would have to say something, I thought, but it turned out the decision had been made for me. The next morning when I went into the backyard, the pot plants had vanished from the roof, and that night for the first time in a week Abicat happily finished his Meow Mix.

College Tour

I was going to college. The only question was where, and since junior year was nearly over, it was time to start looking. Huntingdon College, located three blocks from our house, was out of the running due to being expensive and due to being three blocks from our house. I believed that going a certain distance from home was key to my independence. Though the University of Hawaii had sent what seemed to me a snippy response to my inquiry, I felt that getting out of town was the least I could do.

At this point, Lizzie invited me to go to Judson College to visit her cousin Helen. Lizzie wasn't interested in Auburn, where Ann would be grudgingly graduating in May; she said she wanted a small college.

Judson was small, all right. Located in the exact middle of nowhere, it was a place from which people went to Selma to have a good time. Also, it was a girls' school. According to Helen, students at Judson had the option of dating the cadets from Marion Military Academy, located a stone's throw away, the problem being that Marion only went through sophomore year. Judson girls were then put in the ignominious position of having to date younger and younger guys, possibly winding up with somebody who couldn't drive.

I felt Judson was not for me. Helen probably felt the same way, but she was stuck there. When Mama asked me how the trip had gone, I shook my head.

My next foray was to Mobile. I had met Darlene Monford via the *Star Trek* Alliance, an international club to which I belonged. Things had been grim this spring; *Star Trek* had been canceled. Darlene, in an effort to cheer me up, had invited me to visit her at University of South Alabama which had, she said, an active science fiction club.

Now the problem was getting there. I still didn't drive. This was particularly galling since not only Annette but Patty Harris had their licenses by this time, and Patty had further outdone herself by being given a car for her birthday. It was a Volkswagen Beetle, but still. I hadn't been idle; my attempt to pass the driving exam back in the fall had ended abruptly when I happened to ram the parallel parking car.

I would, I decided, go to Mobile on the bus. Unfortunately, the bus I picked was a local one and stopped at every town with more than 200 people. Finally, we pulled into the Mobile bus station. It was with a sense of relief that I climbed into Darlene's Mercury.

Darlene, who was tall, lanky, and blonde, cherished a passion for the theater as well as science fiction. She was currently starring in the chorus of *Funny Girl* at University of South Alabama and I agreed to go to rehearsal with her the following evening. Meanwhile, we would tour the campus.

South Alabama was a relatively new school. Compared to Judson, which was all red brick buildings and looked like a college, it looked a lot like Sears. The classroom buildings were modern-looking cement cubes. Most of them didn't have windows and they looked a good bit alike. I wondered if people had trouble telling them apart. The dorms were pretty unmistakable, since they were built of concrete block. Fortunately, Darlene lived off campus in a collection of little houses which had been built during World War Two and were now rented out to students.

I felt this was a good sign; having my own place would boost my journey to independence. Darlene and I could even be roommates. Gesturing to a beanbag chair, Darlene invited me to make myself at home. After supper, she added, we would go to a meeting of the science fiction club.

This was more like it. I couldn't imagine Judson having much of a science fiction club.

Darlene made spaghetti and garlic bread, afterwards sticking all the pans into a sink which was already fully occupied with dishes in various degrees of fossilization. "Should I go ahead and wash these?" I asked encouragingly. "Nah, we'll be late. I'll wash them one of these days."

The science fiction club consisted of Darlene, her friend Melanie, whose house was the club headquarters and who was also going to be in *Funny Girl*, and three guys who sat there without saying anything. Everybody agreed that it was a travesty that *Star Trek* was being canceled but nobody knew whether there would be, as rumored, a movie. Melanie provided the entertainment by playing the theme from *2001* on her record player and then reading aloud a story by Isaac Asimov called "What is This Thing Called Love." Then we ate potato chips. When we got back to Darlene's I noticed that her bedroom seemed to be entirely filled by a pile of dirty laundry. I said I would sleep on the couch; I was able to sort of slide its collection of dirty laundry onto the floor.

The next day, we had English muffins for breakfast and I went to Darlene's classes with her. Since she was majoring in theater, these turned out to be interesting. I also perked up a little when somebody mentioned that Dauphin Island, which had a nice beach, was within easy driving distance from campus. If I ever got a car, I could see myself tooling out to the island.

The next excitement would be attending rehearsal. It developed that Darlene and Melanie were in the second line of the chorus and you could see them a good bit of the time. After I congratulated both of them, Darlene dropped me back at her house and said something vague about going to meet a friend, adding that she would see me later.

She never came back. Eventually I got bored, locked all the doors and windows, threw that day's crop of laundry off the couch, and went to sleep. She still wasn't there the next morning. I had two problems: what was for breakfast and how was I getting to the bus station?

There weren't any more English muffins. There wasn't anything else, either, except some Rice Krispies. There wasn't any milk. The closest thing I could find was a bottle of vodka, which I poured over the Krispies. They still crackled.

Just as I was woozily wondering about calling a cab, Darlene showed up. She seemed the worse for wear and was holding her head, but she piled me in the car and we roared off to the bus station.

The bus back to Montgomery was the express so we didn't have to stop except once so everyone could go to the bathroom. Mama met me at the terminal. "Well?" she asked eagerly. I shook my head.

At this point, Lizzie weighed in again. What about University of Montevallo? It was located within easy driving distance of the bright lights of Birmingham, but it was a small school, it was coed and the price was right. Four of us drove up including Annette DeSalvo and Edna Joy Joyner, who went by "Eddie." I had thought Annette would follow Hal to University of Alabama, but she said Hal had dissuaded her, saying Alabama was too hard and she would only embarrass her family by flunking out.

"Right," I said, my usual response whenever anybody said anything stupid.

Montevallo was architecturally interesting. The streets were of brick and so were most of the buildings, including the enormous Main Dorm. This dorm had the oddest fire escapes I had ever seen. They were like big metal tubes, each containing a spiral slide, affixed to the side of the building. I could imagine whizzing merrily down the tube; clearly the place had some entertainment value, especially compared to Judson.

We were being toured around by Lois, a freshman who was thinking of majoring in geology. She marched us across campus to the science building. "We have a geode," she said helpfully.

I was interested. I was a big fan of geodes, which look like rocks until you get somebody to saw one open, at which time the rock turns out to be hollow and lined with magnificent crystals. Montevallo probably had a pretty nice geode, I thought; maybe something about the size of a bowling ball.

Lois led us into a courtyard. Strategically poised at its center was a big pedestal supporting an enormous geode. It was big enough to sit in. It wasn't lined with crystals but with a sort of iridescent ore. A highway crew had found it while building the Interstate, said Lois, and the entire building had been designed around the geode to keep anybody from stealing it. I didn't think there was any danger of that unless the thief had come equipped with a forklift, but I had to admit I was impressed. Not only had I never seen a geode that big, I strongly suspected that nobody had ever seen a geode that big.

When I got home, Mama said "Well?" and I nodded.

The Bus to Europe

It was summer, 1969. The astronauts were going to the moon. More remarkably, I was going to Europe. There was apparently no end to the benefits conferred on my family by the settlement of The Texas Case. There had been enough money for Mama to remodel the attic, so that I had a bathroom, and for her to acquire a used car and the carport to house it. Now it developed that there was enough money for us to go on a three week bus tour of Europe.

There was one problem: what would we do about Abicat? The solution arrived in the form of Mrs. Tate, one of Mama's needy old ladies. Mrs. Tate raised Persian cats. She could board Abi for three weeks, she said. I wondered how Abi would feel about this. Caged up with a bunch of pregnant Persians, he would probably assume that he had been unjustly sentenced to some sort of feline maternity version of Sing Sing.

Abicat aside, I had qualms about the language barrier. I was taking Spanish but a fat lot of good that would do since we weren't going to Spain. I finally got a French phrase book and mastered asking for the bathroom. (The phrase was helpfully rendered phonetically: Oo Aye la Doobla Va Say? They didn't tell you how to understand the answer.)

A couple of days before we left, Apollo 11 landed and I went to Patty Harris' for a Moon Party. Everybody sat on the floor in front of the television to watch Neil Armstrong climb down the ladder. There had been some controversy about whether the moon was about twenty feet deep in moon dust, so we were all relieved that the lunar lander hadn't sunk out of sight. Armstrong hopped off the bottom rung, recovered his wits, and delivered himself of his epic pronouncement: "That's one small step for a man, one giant leap for mankind."

I thought "Really? You land on the moon and the only thing you can come up with is something along the lines of 'Winston Tastes Good Like a Cigarette Should'?"

Armstrong's limitations as a public speaker notwithstanding, humans had reached the moon.

We went outside and lit sparklers under the full moon. I wasn't sure why they had had to wait until it was full, since I did understand that the moon remained the same size all month.

Then we were off to Europe. Our first stop was New York City, where we saw the Empire State Building and where Ray and Clay got in trouble at the hotel for an incident involving water balloons. The city was full of billboards advertising *Fiddler on the Roof*. Clay was unimpressed, saying he was not about to pay money to see some guy hopping from roof to roof with a fiddle.

Our flight to London was happily uneventful and the next morning we showed up in the hotel lobby, thoroughly jet lagged, to meet the group we would be living with for the next three weeks. This is when we met Tommy and Plotnick.

Tommy and Martha Ann Turner were from Beaufort, South Carolina. This was their first trip to Europe. Marvin and Blanche Plotnick were from Brooklyn. This was apparently their first trip anywhere. They were accompanied by Blanche's mother, Mrs. Rattner, who Plotnick addressed as Ma, and their daughter Joyce, who was my age and wore false eyelashes. Nobody called Plotnick by his first name; even Blanche just addressed him as "hey."

Plotnick and Tommy took one look at each other and became inseparable. It was possible that they were each thinking that they had never met anyone like that. I'd never met anybody like Plotnick either. The closest I'd gotten was by watching *The Honeymooners*, or maybe Phil Silvers.

In addition to the Plotnicks and Turners, the group ran heavily to teachers and a group of rather loud girls from Texas, to whom Joyce immediately gravitated. The tour leader was a young German guy named Volker who said he was headed to law school in the fall. I gave him a commiserating look.

Everybody on the bus had seen the movie *If It's Tuesday, This Must Be Belgium*, so we were sort of ready for anything, but I was still rather taken aback by the food.

In England, I had been unpleasantly surprised to find that they put butter on their sandwiches, when it seemed to me that mustard would have made more sense. Plotnick had a lot more trouble with the food than I did, though. He kept asking if the dish before him was kosher, and, being met with a blank look, would sigh.

The food situation improved in Switzerland, where I discovered fondue. We ate to the accompaniment of yodeling, which didn't add to the experience, but the fondue itself was great. After a whispered consultation with the waiter, even Plotnick dug in.

One of the most interesting things about Plotnick was the way Blanche gave him hell. At one point, he had become convinced they should rent a car. God knows why, since the bus was already paid for. Blanche wasn't in favor of the idea. As she put it, in the hotel lobby and at the top of her voice, "We don't need no cah, ya stoopid idiot bastid." We all watched, enthralled, to see if Plotnick's response would involve gunfire, but he seemed to take the incident in stride. They didn't rent a car; the only fallout from the event came later that day when Ray found himself in the elevator with Plotnick, who said "Never get married, kid. Take it from me." Later the couple got in a fight in front of the Eiffel Tower over whether Plotnick's photo had done the monument justice.

I was having some trouble with the language, though not as much as Clay, who wasn't very proficient in English either. Right after we left France for Belgium, Mama had been reviewing the fact that in France they spoke French. Clay was interested enough to offer a comment: "What they speak here? Belch?" The reaction to his remark offended him so much that he quit talking altogether.

We crossed into Italy, where we were supposed to visit Venice. Mama had been looking forward to it, but on that morning Ray was sick. He had managed his insulin shots satisfactorily until then. Unfortunately, he had become overconfident enough to consume most of a bottle of wine. Mama had to stay behind with him and summon a doctor, who spoke as much English as we did Italian. The doctor, through pantomime, indicated that he didn't know what the hell was wrong with Ray, but suggested he wear a flannel undershirt to keep his stomach warm.

Weirdly, this sort of worked.

By missing Venice, however, Mama and Ray missed the most exciting Plotnick episode of the trip. After we finished touring St. Mark's Square, we had returned to the mainland parking lot along with a whole busload of Japanese tourists. When they got on their bus, so did Ma. Admittedly, the buses looked alike. "Ma!" yelled Tommy and Plotnick in unison, pursuing the departing bus. Through the back window, Mrs. Rattner could dimly be seen, surrounded by Japanese people taking pictures. Fortunately, Volker was able to call ahead and get the bus halted. With her mother restored to her, Blanche summed up the entire incident: "Ah fa Godsake."

In Rome, we were suitably wowed by the immensity of the Vatican. However, Ray and Clay were even more interested in the ruins of the Colosseum, in which several hundred cats seemed to be living. My brothers may have been motivated by missing Abicat; at any rate they climbed down in there and were happily petting cats at random when they were observed by the police, whom they handily outdistanced. I was duly appalled to note that, in addition to ruins and cats, Rome was overflowing with hippies. They were everywhere you looked. In fact, the Spanish Steps were apparently the European headquarters for hippies. There were acres of them, sprawling peacefully, playing the occasional guitar. The Romans didn't seem to mind, probably because they had already become accustomed to the cats.

Eventually, it was time to leave. On the flight back, the pilot announced we would be flying over Woodstock, New York, where a huge rock festival was in progress. More hippies. I was more concerned with the tailwinds from Hurricane Camille, which had blasted the Mississippi Gulf Coast and which now made the plane bounce alarmingly.

Back at home, we bailed out Abicat, who was overjoyed at having made parole. I had grown an inch and could now speak bathroom-related phrases in several languages. I knew about fondue. I had seen an Alp, the Empire State Building, and hippies. I was, I thought, ready for senior year.

That December, we sent a Christmas card to the Turners and made a special trip to the Hallmark store in Normandale to get a Hanukah card for Plotnick. We addressed it to Marvin and Blanche in case they were still married.

Lunch Table

By the time I was a senior, Lanier was pretty well integrated, at least at my lunch table.

In fact, everybody but me was black.

Dessa Hall, who sat next to me, was a mysterious presence. She always seemed rather sad about something, and was given to looking around the lunchroom and sighing. I couldn't blame her, though I thought it probably had something to do with the food and was thus not my problem. I brought my lunch, which Mama packed every morning while she packed hers. We always had the same thing, pimiento cheese sandwiches wrapped in the tin foil we had saved from the previous day.

Next to Dessa sat Jackaline Dallas. An Air Force kid, she seemed temperamentally the opposite of Dessa and inclined to be talkative; at our first lunchtime, she had stated that she had been named for both her parents, Jackson and Idaline Dallas. At the end of the table sat Stella Blue, who was always referred to as Stella Blue. I had no idea whether Blue was her middle name, her last name or some sort of moniker like Baby Face Nelson. Stella was always stylishly dressed, sported fake fingernails (and, whispered Jackaline, fake hair) and was inclined to discuss her social life. Her tendency to overshare was one of the few things that cheered Dessa up, since it gave her and Jackaline an opportunity to insult Stella's taste in men whenever Stella left the table.

Jackaline was inclined to be friendly, though she had one bad fixation: she thought all white people were rich. I felt that somebody living on an air base where gasoline was only 25 cents a gallon and where, for all I knew, everything else was probably free, really had no business calling somebody who was having to re-use tin foil rich.

In order to counter the prevailing, and accurate, assumption that the white students were unfriendly, I decided it was up to me to keep the conversational ball rolling at lunch. Music was a reliable topic; once even Dessa perked up when Jackaline mentioned the Jackson Five. We could also discuss television, though to keep up with the conversation it was necessary to know the names of all the *Soul Train* dancers. Jackaline also enjoyed discussing politics, though her main contribution to the subject consisted of acquiring a bumper sticker from one of George Wallace's campaigns and demonstrating how it could be cut up and the letters rearranged to spell CALL ME.

Occasionally, we discussed our plans for after high school. Dessa and I were going to college.

Jackaline's father expected her to join the Air Force; she was undecided since, as she put it, she did not want to get her booty shot off. Stella Blue's plans were on hold; after she left to put up her tray, Jackaline and Dessa offered the theory that Stella's plans undoubtedly involved separating some fool from his paycheck.

Occasionally Dessa would show a flash of animation, once announcing apropos of nothing that her father was a private detective. "Wow!" I said, imagining somebody like Humphrey Bogart. I figured suppertime conversation at Dessa's house must feature a daily recap of how Mr. Hall had spent the afternoon filling some stool pigeon full of lead. Dessa had clearly won the most interesting father contest. Jackaline's father was a sergeant, mine was dead, and Stella Blue was uncertain as to her father's current occupation and whereabouts, stating that he was off doing his thing somewhere. I hadn't said anything about my father having been a lawyer since that would have been certain to set Jackaline off.

Despite having an interesting father, Dessa remained somewhat abstracted; this was odd since it was actually a rather exciting time of year. Homecoming was just around the corner, and we were voting for our favorite teens to represent the class of 1970. The campaigning was intense; the cheerleaders weren't speaking to each other. The only contest not in doubt was for the title of Most Lanierish, for which a girl named Hobson Lanier was felt to be a shoo-in.

The school play was in production, too. For some reason, the drama department, which prided itself on picking uplifting works, had selected *Li'l Abner*. I wasn't sure how a stage full of hillbillies was supposed to improve our self-esteem.

Maybe they thought we'd look good in comparison.

One day at lunch, Jackaline had asked Dessa if she was interested in going to the play.

"No," said Dessa shortly. "Because it's snow white."

"No it's not," said Jackaline reassuringly. "It's *Li'l Abner*. The one with the hillbillies."

I fell out of my chair laughing; Dessa stated that she meant that all the cast members were white.

I was about to point out that so were the vast majority of hillbillies when Dessa finally decided to unburden herself. Up until the current year, she announced, she had been a student at Booker T. Washington High School, which she referred to as Booker Washington. The school's physical plant had had some problems, she conceded. The heat never worked, the roof leaked, and a chunk of the science lab ceiling had once turned loose, beaning her cousin Ima.

Nevertheless, Booker Washington was a paradise compared to what, gesturing, she referred to despairingly as "This Place." At Booker Washington, she had been a hit in school plays, had belonged to all the major clubs, and had been a Homecoming Princess. This year, she continued grimly, she would certainly have made Homecoming Court, and possibly Miss Washington, had an unkind fate not teamed up with the school board to exile her to a place where she did not have, as she put it, a snowball's chance and where she was subjected to any number of daily indignities.

I tried to cheer her up by pointing out that I wasn't going to be a Homecoming Princess either, but she merely gave me a look which made me wonder whether lunching with me was one of the daily indignities.

Gloom reigned; even Jackaline looked relatively sad. A change of subject was, I felt, in order.

"Well, at least," I said, "you don't have to live in a haunted house."

This statement created a gratifying sensation.

"What???" said Dessa, dropping her fork.

"Your house is haunted? Really?" said Jackaline.

"Well, yeah," I said. "It's my grandmother. The other night I was going upstairs—"

"You have a upstairs," said Jackaline accusingly. "See, only rich people—"

I gave her the sort of look Dessa usually reserved for me. Dessa, meanwhile, had scooted her chair back and was looking uneasy. "It's only my grandmother," I said with some asperity. "I mean, it's not as if it was that guy in the dining room—"

"What guy? What dining room?" said Dessa, scooting her chair farther back.

"See, you got a dining room—" said Jackaline.

"Guy in the dining room," I repeated, louder. "The guy that built our house supposedly went in the dining room and shot himself—"

Dessa quietly rose, picked up her purse, and appeared to be calculating the distance to the fire door.

"What he shoot himself?" asked Jackaline.

"Well, I don't know but maybe he'd lost his money."

"See—" said Jackaline.

At this point the situation, whatever it was, resolved itself with the noisy arrival of Stella Blue, who plunked her tray down and announced that on Friday, she would be at the Midtown Holiday Inn, attending a party so exclusive that it would cost 50 cents to get in the door.

Dessa sat back down. In unison, she and Jackaline informed Stella Blue that they personally would not be fool enough to go to any party where you had to pay money.

Stella Blue retorted that she would not be the one paying the money, since she would be attending the party at the express invitation of Arthur Robinson.

Dessa and Jackaline considered this. Finally, Dessa spoke up. "The light Arthur Robinson or the dark Arthur Robinson?"

Since I didn't know either Arthur Robinson, I felt uniquely unqualified to critique Stella Blue's choice of party escorts. Besides, I'd finished my sandwich. I folded my tinfoil and put it in my purse, checking first to make sure the cheesy side of the foil wasn't outermost.

As I went up to the garbage can with my tattered and unreusable paper bag, I considered. Obviously, information about my homelife, however interesting, wasn't going to cheer anybody up.

Maybe we should just go back to talking politics.

Grapevine

Whenever Jackaline annoyed me by claiming that I must be rich since I was white, I would play my trump card, informing the lunch table at large that at least none of them had to have a part-time job. It was true; every day after lunch I went to my job at Blount Brothers Construction.

I never mentioned the fact that I was only working to get out of afternoon study hall. Housed in the cavernous school auditorium, a shadowy place built to hold hundreds of students, study hall was impossible to police; even if you called in the National Guard, which would not have been a bad idea, the place would still have been a smorgasbord of violence.

When a rumor spread that the resident mob of study hall hoodlums had armed themselves with knives in addition to their usual rubber bands and spitballs, I decided to avail myself of the Diversified Office Occupations program, which fixed me up with my part-time job as a typist.

Not only was I only going to half as much school as everybody else, I was getting paid for the privilege. I was enjoying the best of all possible worlds, though getting there hadn't been easy. My first job interview was for a position with Jackson Hospital, where I had been born. I thought this fact would render me a shoo-in, but I wasn't offered the job. I was upset until Dana Sue Oliver, who had gotten hired in my place, told me that her new boss was a psycho who had hurled a wastebasket at her.

In addition to getting out of study hall, my job afforded me the funds to get Mama a dishwasher. Since our house had been built in 1920, it lacked modern amenities, and there was no chance that what little was left of The Texas Case funds would cover the plumbing alterations that a built-in dishwasher required. Right after I started work, though, I noticed that Sears was selling a portable dishwasher designed to be attached to the kitchen sink faucet. The fact that it was on sale for $79 pretty much clinched the deal. I was able to talk Annette's mother into putting it on her Sears card, with the promise that I would pay for it out of my first paycheck. I foresaw an ideal

Christmas present for Mama: practical as well as spectacular.

Now my only problem was the party drought.

Along with the rest of the lunch table, I loved "I Heard it Through the Grapevine." The Marvin Gaye version, not the other one. I was always on the lookout for a party so I could dance to my favorite tune.

I hadn't had a whole lot of luck with dances, at which they tended not to play "I Heard it Through the Grapevine." Besides that, I had trouble keeping up with the latest dance crazes; they were always changing and nobody could be sure they were doing them right. In the case of the bugaloo, nobody was even sure how to spell it. At parties, people tended to be less judgmental. Somebody was bound to bring a record player and a stack of records, and if they forgot, you could try the radio; WHHY was pretty reliable as far as playing "I Heard it Through the Grapevine" at least once per hour.

So far this fall, nobody was having parties. It wasn't just me; the people at my job said the same thing.

Working at Blount Brothers was fairly entertaining, and less dangerous than school or the hospital. The job wasn't likely to improve my social life, though. My fellow part-time workers were friendly but there wasn't much chance of either of them throwing a party. Gladys belonged to the Pentecostal Holiness church, which was dead set against parties, and Mary Susan spent every leisure moment with Ronnie, her fiance. She talked a lot about Ronnie, whose only fault seemed to be that he had the Bride of Frankenstein for a mother.

I was afraid my senior year might turn out to be boring. My co-workers had been pretty excited about the South Alabama Fair, but I wasn't all that interested, since the fair didn't count as a party and since it was raining that day. Besides that, the event got loused up by Mary Susan, who, Gladys reported, had thrown her engagement ring at Ronnie and told him to give it to his mother. This was a blow to office morale and had implications at school, since Ronnie was in the Diversified Office Occupations class with me, Gladys, and Mary Susan. In fact, Ronnie and Mary Susan had been sitting together until the Monday after the fair, when Mary Susan ostentatiously told me to change seats with her. Ronnie seemed pretty blue. "I don't know what I done," he said miserably. I tried to cheer him up by saying I was pretty sure Mary Susan would tell him eventually.

In fact, Mary Susan filled him in before the end of the week, accusing Ronnie's mother of trying to ruin their wedding, set for June, by insisting that they serve a type of punch made from lime sherbet and 7-Up which, according to Gladys, Mary Susan claimed would clash with the avocado green bridesmaid dresses and which furthermore looked like paint.

I had been to weddings featuring this stuff, and it pretty much tasted like paint, too.

Paint or no paint, the story had a happy ending. Even though Mary Susan was now referring to her future mother-in-law as Lady MacBeth, Ronnie had decided that he and Mary Susan should elope, so one weekend after Thanksgiving they ran off to Georgia and were married by a judge. I got them a *Betty Crocker Cookbook*.

Things quieted down after that; the only immediate repercussion was that Mrs. Travers, the DOO teacher, told Mary Susan that she couldn't sign her test papers "Mrs. Ronnie Strickland" even though Mary Susan insisted that it was now her legal name. The newlyweds, who were living with Ronnie's grandfather, were back to sitting together, and the atmosphere at work improved accordingly.

To top things off, the DOO students were getting ready to have their Christmas party, at which there was guaranteed to be dancing, and "I Heard it Through the Grapevine" was obviously going to be featured. As they said on *American Bandstand*, it had a great beat and was easy to dance to. My only quandary involved what to wear. I had recently sewn myself an outfit that the *Butterick Pattern Book* referred to as Party Pajamas—a sort of festive jumpsuit. Though it was colorful as well as stylish, featuring a design of large blue roses, I felt a little uneasy about wearing it, since somebody at the party might recognize the fabric as having come from a bolt of drapery material. Luckily, I developed a backup plan which I was sure would make me the star of the party.

I got a paper dress.

I had ordered this dress from the Alcoa Company for four dollars and a Reynolds Wrap box top.

Despite the name, my dress was not made of paper or foil, but of some silvery material which probably included a lot of plastic. It had shoulder straps and was originally floor length, but I had customized it with a pair of scissors so that it now consisted mostly of fringe up to mid-thigh.

DOO's college-bound contingent was made up of me and a guy named Johnny Barber, so I was already pretty famous, and I figured showing up in a paper dress would secure my popularity for all time.

The party was held in the conference room of a downtown hotel. I wobbled a little as I swished into the room, since I was wearing a pair of Mama's old high heels—the sort with ankle straps. I had spray-painted the shoes silver, and except for the fact that some paint had come off on my feet, I felt I looked pretty close to the height of teen fashion. Besides that, I was going to ditch the shoes as soon as I made my entrance.

The party had not exactly taken off yet. In fact, a lot of the students were just sitting around looking through a pile of old yearbooks one of the teachers had brought; the styles of ten years ago were always good for a laugh. "Yeah! Strapless dresses!" I chortled, pointing to a photo of a taffeta-clad prom queen whose dress was inflated by at least ten crinolines. "Can you believe anybody would actually wear that?" Fringe flapping, I rustled over to the record player, where I was pleased to see "I Heard it Through the Grapevine" topping the pile of .45s. I sat on a folding chair to undo my ankle straps, then tossed the shoes into a corner.

"Crank it up!" I said happily.

"We can't," said Dana Sue Oliver. "Somebody forgot the spindle."

This was a low blow. The record player came with a thin center spindle suitable for playing albums. The only way to play a .45 was to use a thick auxiliary spindle, which some jerk had forgotten to bring. The party's musical entertainment now consisted solely of *Top Forty Solid Gold*, albums one through twelve.

Dana Sue cranked it up anyway.

"Shimmy Shimmy Koko Bop."

I sat back down.

Mr. Thompson

Mr. Thompson was not the first black teacher I'd had, since in junior year I had been in Mrs. Lawrence's social studies class. A thin, sad woman, Mrs. Lawrence seemed to consider us her cross to bear. The first day of class she had asked us to indicate which direction west was, and nobody knew.

Things never got much better. Though we refrained from behaving abysmally toward Mrs. Lawrence, feeling that she had suffered enough, we did laugh heartily whenever she became flustered and said something funny. Once, while pointing out that the Gettysburg Address had received only a lukewarm reception in its time, she said sadly, "Abraham Lincoln was dead and in his grave before he realized he'd written a masterpiece." That was pretty much the highlight of the semester.

In the fall of senior year, I had Mr. Thompson for American Government. The first day, he had introduced himself as George W. Thompson and said that he'd been in the military and that we could check his qualifications if there was any doubt. He seemed nervous. I couldn't think why—surely he'd been given combat training. He may have consulted with Mrs. Lawrence; at any rate he didn't ask us to name the cardinal directions.

Despite any initial misgivings on everyone's part, after the first Parent-Teacher Night Open House, our relationship with Mr. Thompson was on a solid footing. Apparently all the students' parents or other relatives had turned out; Mr. Thompson had been bowled over by the attendance and expressed himself as being both humble and proud of the show of support.

In fact, after Parent-Teacher Night, Mr. Thompson turned out to be one of the most entertaining teachers any of us had ever had. While discussing the doctrine of separation of church and state, he decided to reference King Henry the Eighth's dissolution of the monasteries. In recounting the misadventures of the king and Anne Boleyn, Mr. Thompson apparently felt that the material would be more compelling if he acted the whole thing out, doing all the voices.

"King Henry sees Anne Boleyn," he reported, "And his head go round and round. He says, 'Bring Me That Woman.'"

He then switched perspectives. "Anne Boleyn says, 'Look here, King. I will not stoop to your whims and whams.'" He admired Anne Boleyn's strength of character, though he acknowledged that it hadn't done her much good.

Occasionally Mr. Thompson would illustrate a point with a scene from his own childhood. We were still on separation of church and state when he mentioned that he had gone to a one-room school where the teacher began the day by making each student say a Bible verse. No one was allowed to repeat a verse. There was in Mr. Thompson's class a boy named Leroy, who through flunking several years in a row was now bigger and meaner than anybody in the class, including the teacher. Leroy had selected "Jesus wept," as his own personal Bible verse; no one else was allowed to say it under pain of dismemberment. Mr. Thompson, who sat right in front of Leroy, was one day seized with a death wish. As he put it, when called on for his Bible verse, he said "Hee hee hee Jesus wept."

Leroy, down but not out, said in his turn "Uh, uh, He Sho Did."

Fortunately, Mr. Thompson had planned his exit strategy. When class was dismissed, he jumped out the window and took off cross country. Although Leroy eventually caught up with him, Mr. Thompson felt that the fame it brought him made the entire incident worthwhile.

In October, I was able to approach Mr. Thompson with a problem which I felt only he could solve. Jimmy Cates was running for reelection to the state legislature. He had recently been horrified to discover that his name had been left off the Yellow Paper, a sample ballot distributed in the black community with the names of candidates who were felt to be sympathetic to black concerns. Many people in the black community took the Yellow Paper with them to the polls. Being left off the list boded ill for any candidate. When I told Mr. Thompson that Jimmy Cates had been left off despite what seemed a sterling record in the legislature, Mr. Thompson had responded that he was attending a voters' meeting that very night and that he would report the omission. Jimmy Cates got beaten anyway, but I felt at least we'd tried.

Sometimes Mr. Thompson brooded over conditions at Lanier. After a run-in with the old harridan who ran the library, and whose main career goal was to prevent people from reading the books, he stated somberly "It takes an act of Congress to check out a book from this library." His own experience made him sympathetic to Ray, who was starting high school that year and was prone to cut class. One day Ray had dropped by just as class was ending. I introduced Ray to Mr. Thompson, adding that Ray was skipping school. "I don't blame you," said Mr. Thompson sincerely.

Once in a while, Mr. Thompson had a run-in with a student. A very thin black girl named Lucinda sat in front of me. She had an enormous Afro which made her resemble a chrysanthemum. Apparently Lucinda had suggested to Mr. Thompson that he should give the black students in the class better grades in order to show solidarity. Mr. Thompson was not amused. "I don't care if you are green," he said solemnly.

He was also somewhat concerned with some of the students' reactions to the news of the My Lai massacre in Viet Nam, which we didn't hear about until late fall. Melissa Arnold, who was from one of the military families, felt that people were making a big deal about nothing. She explained that Vietnamese people weren't like us and didn't really mind if somebody killed their families. Mr. Thompson shook his head. "Miss Arnold," he said sadly, "you are bloodthirsty."

Mr. Thompson had one big advantage over Mrs. Lawrence; by the time we met him, the movie *To Sir With Love* had been released. This movie, which starred Sidney Poitier, involved a black teacher in a London slum who eventually wins the hearts of his students, who call him Sir. The movie also starred Lulu, a short pudgy British pop star. At the end of the movie, the students present Sidney Poitier a trophy engraved "To Sir with Love," after which Lulu sings.

As the spring semester started, it was felt that we should do something special for Mr. Thompson. The idea of giving him an engraved trophy was proposed and immediately shouted down on the grounds it would cost money. We briefly considered calling him Sir, but concluded that he would probably just think we had all gone insane. Finally, Melissa Arnold, who didn't hold a grudge from being called bloodthirsty, said we should give him a surprise birthday party. This was a good idea. It wouldn't cost anywhere near as much as a trophy, it would get us out of class, and we could eat the cake. Furthermore, said

Melissa, she knew when Mr. Thompson's birthday was because she had asked Mrs. Palmer.

Mrs. Palmer was also black and something of a heroine to the female students, because once in her class one of the black guys had advanced the theory that the birth control pill was a plot on the part of white people to wipe out the black race. Mrs. Palmer had lit into him and said she doubted if he could find any black women who thought that. As a committed feminist, Mrs. Palmer was obviously the ideal person to help us plan a birthday party.

The party itself was easy enough to organize; everybody contributed a dollar and Melissa ordered a cake from the bakery on the air base. The problem was getting Mr. Thompson out of the room so we could set things up and arrange the decorations.

A distraction was called for, and Mrs. Palmer volunteered.

Meanwhile, I had to decide what to wear. I finally settled on an outfit which would include a vest of which I was particularly proud. Made of suede, it featured fringe which started at the bosom and cascaded riotously all the way to the ankles. As I swished my way to class, I was happy to see Mrs. Palmer propelling Mr. Thompson down the hall, her arm linked in his, chattering vivaciously. He looked confused, but she succeeded in dragging him off in the opposite direction from the classroom while we got the cake and paper plates arranged and wrote Happy Birthday on the blackboard. Finally, after the bell had actually rung, Mr. Thompson appeared looking somewhat nonplussed. "Poor Mrs. Palmer," he announced, "has lost her mind."

Then he noticed the balloons. Nobody sang "To Sir with Love," but the party was a great success. Mrs. Palmer appeared in time to have a slice of cake. The bakery had, in fact, outdone itself. One cake layer was vanilla; the other chocolate. Mr. Thompson beamed. "Integrated cake," he said.

Elvis

Annette DeSalvo always wanted to go see Elvis movies. This was sort of a pain, since Elvis and I had a troubled history going way back.

I thought "Hound Dog" was the stupidest song I had ever heard in my life. At the time, my life consisted of only four years, but still. There was Elvis Presley, on television, acting like a complete idiot. He compounded the felony some time later by appearing on an album cover wearing a solid gold suit. I saw this album in Loveman's Department Store and thought that Elvis had hit a new low, even for him. "Is Elvis Presley tacky?" I had asked Mama."Yes, he's very tacky," said Mama reassuringly.

There was one person whose musical tastes were so low that she was guaranteed to like Elvis. That was my half-sister Mona. Mona had been adopted by my father and Cammie, his first wife. According to Mama, my father had been in the market for a baby when a woman he knew coincidentally turned up with one she didn't need. It didn't occur to me until later to be suspicious of the timing.

Since Cammie and my father had divorced when Mona was little, we only saw her a couple of times a year. She would arrive on the bus from Columbus, Mississippi, accompanied by a ukulele, a record player and an enormous number of crinoline petticoats. Mona was crazy about Elvis. In addition to "Hound Dog," she was a big fan of "Blue Suede Shoes," which I thought was the second-stupidest song I had ever heard. Things got so bad that if I was trying to have a race with the rest of the neighborhood kids, we couldn't even start running until Mona had intoned "One for the money! Two for the show! Three to get ready! Go cat go!"

After Mona blew into town, you couldn't walk past the radio without getting a dose of Elvis. These Elvis songs were particularly galling because they completely replaced the music I had been listening to. I had been fond of a song with the catchy phrase "Jeepers Creepers where'd you get those peepers," which I usually rendered as "where'd you get those sneakers," since that made more sense. Following the Elvis invasion, I could forget about "Jeepers Creepers." Even after Mona packed up her ukulele and got back on the bus, the Elvis bombardment continued.

I was getting really tired of it, when there came the announcement that Elvis had been drafted. Serves him right, I thought bitterly.

After that, there was a lull of several years, ushered in partly by the fact that Mona had suddenly gotten married. We heard from her sporadically and from Elvis not at all, until Elvis decided to go into movies and Annette announced she had a crush on him.

It was Mona all over again. Since Annette was officially my best friend, I got dragged along to see *Viva Las Vegas*, *Follow that Dream*, and *Jailhouse Rock*, the only one I really liked since I thought there was a chance Elvis might actually land in jail.

The other movie I didn't mind was *Blue Hawaii*. It was not half bad, and it was possible to concentrate on the scenery and sort of ignore Elvis. I hoped Elvis would go on to make more movies in the same vein, maybe *Blue Bermuda*, and eventually he did come out with *Paradise Hawaiian Style* but unfortunately right after that he decided to become relevant.

According to the photos Annette had posted on her bedroom wall, he had grown sideburns and started wearing satin jumpsuits for his shows. Annette still faithfully bought his records, even though the songs now included numbers like "In the Ghetto" which was about somebody getting shot and was not easy to dance to.

Around this time Elvis got married and I thought that would discourage Annette, but all she did was start teasing her hair so she would look more like Priscilla Presley, who was in fact not much older than we were. This presented me with a quandary. Since Annette was my official best friend I was pretty much committed to doing whatever she did. The fact that she was four months older settled it. I started teasing my hair, but it didn't seem to do much good.

By this time, Annette was dating Hal 9000 and I felt that he was not going to sit still for her having a crush on someone else, but he didn't seem at all bothered, probably because Elvis was in Hollywood and we weren't.

Then Annette escalated matters by deciding that her lifetime goal was to see Elvis in person. I didn't think there was much chance of that. Elvis wasn't going to appear for the local radio station's Big Bam Show or anything lame like that. I supposed it was barely possible that Annette could wind up going to Memphis to tour Graceland but her parents weren't keen on the idea. If Hal had found out about her plan, he wouldn't have been in favor of it either, but that was a moot point since for the foreseeable future Annette was stuck in Montgomery. Until she learned how to drive her non-film options were pretty much limited to following Elvis via movie magazines, one of which had done a full-color photo spread of his Las Vegas wedding featuring the largest cake I had ever seen. Meanwhile, the Elvis movies continued to pour out of Hollywood.

I sat through *Clambake, Speedway,* and *The Trouble with Girls* before Elvis' film career took what I hoped would be its final dive. In the fall of my senior year, Elvis came out with a movie called *Change of Habit*, in which he played a ghetto doctor and Mary Tyler Moore played a ghetto nun who is working incognito to preserve her secret identity and with whom Elvis falls in love. "He's getting obsessed with this ghetto business," I thought, but I felt pretty cheerful because I thought I could see the light at the end of the tunnel. Annette's family was Catholic and she went to Our Lady Queen of Sorrows with Patty Harris and Patty's mother Clara, who was officially crazy and who kept up with all the movies that the Vatican said were blasphemous.

Patty hadn't been allowed to go with me to see *Li'l Abner* on grounds of blasphemy and I felt that an Elvis movie where he falls in love with a nun would certainly make the list, especially in light of Elvis' previous history with *Jailhouse Rock*.

I was completely outflanked by Clara, though, who had been such a fan of Debbie Reynolds in *The Singing Nun* that she had bought the album. Apparently nuns weren't blasphemous even if they were incognito and hanging around Elvis.

To add insult to injury, Clara insisted on coming to the movie with Patty, Annette, and me.

Annette rolled her eyes pretty much nonstop on the drive over, but she was capable of seeing the silver lining. "Just wait," she said, "I'm getting a car for my birthday and after that, we'll go to the show without Clara."

I was envious. I didn't see how I was even going to get my driver's license since despite practicing I still found it impossible to parallel park. Nevertheless, once Annette got her car I was always happy to ride with her to get a frozen Coke. We were en route to Pak-a-Sak one day when she said, all excited, "Guess what??"

I was afraid to guess, but it turned out Annette was going to drive to Birmingham to visit one of her hundreds of cousins. This was cool enough, but it paled in comparison to what came next. "And then my cousin Teresa Maria and me are going to drive to Houston to see Elvis!"

I wondered what Hal would say, but he was away at college and it was highly probable that she hadn't filled him in on the plan. I was sort of worried she was going to invite me, but I guess she decided blood was thicker than water because she didn't.

I told Annette I was happy for her, but in fact I thought that seeing Elvis in person would make her intolerable. She was already bad enough even though she had stopped carrying an Elvis notebook to school.

I was expecting to hear from Annette the minute she got back from Houston but in fact it was the following Saturday when she called to ask if I wanted to get a Coke. We had gotten halfway to Pak-a-Sak before I blurted out "Well? How was Elvis?" There was a silence before she said, shortly, "Fat. He's gotten fat. He had on a jumpsuit and you could see his stomach stick out."

The next time I saw her room, she had replaced Elvis with Fess Parker.

I smiled. Elvis had left the building.

Underground

I don't know whose idea it was to start an underground newspaper, but the staff wound up being me, Eddie Joyner, and three guys. Dave Currens and Rick Smaltz were both intellectuals. Harold Jeffrey, who had appointed himself editor, was more of a jerk, but he had a mimeograph machine.

Eddie had started out with aspirations to the theater, but abandoned her career in the Lanier drama department after it turned out that her only role senior year involved serving as understudy to the girl who played Mammy Yokum. Instead, she was concentrating on feminist issues and had agreed to serve on the paper since she felt it would be a springboard to her career as a college activist. She in turn had talked me into writing for the paper, saying I would be a natural since I was already on the staff of the *North Tower.*

First, though, we had to pick out a name. We settled on *The Truth*, which we felt would grab readers. We worried that we would have trouble with the administration, which weighed in on pretty much every aspect of life at Lanier, but they didn't seem to notice that we existed.

We had decided that we would be the counter culture answer to the official Lanier paper, the *Blue and White*, but that we wouldn't bother covering obvious things like the football team's string of victories. We would cover the really important stories, like the Yippies' stance against the war and pay toilets. I thought this was a great idea for a story, especially the part about pay toilets, and in fact the article I submitted anonymously appeared under the byline I.P. Freely.

We didn't have a place to meet at school, since we were a radical underground newspaper, so our headquarters was Eddie's house. This worked out great since her mother baked a mean cookie. Besides that, Eddie's father was an actual newspaper reporter and he was always around to offer advice about not letting the system get us down. The reason he was always around was that he had lost his job, the system having gotten him down.

My main problem was getting Harold Jeffrey, who was always addressed as Jeffrey, to agree that my ideas for stories were obviously superior to whatever he had thought up. During spring semester, the Apollo 13 moon shot had run into serious trouble on the way to the moon, and in fact had to turn around and concentrate on getting back to Earth. I didn't think *The Truth* was fully on top of the crisis.

Apollo 13 was a really big story, I argued, and in fact would lend itself to a whole series about what happens when people disrespect the number thirteen. One question that obviously needed to be asked: if they don't have thirteenth floors in hotels, what made NASA think it was a good idea to use the number for a spaceship?

Jeffrey was adamant that the paper, which we had just voted to rename the *First Amendment*, should devote its front page to his exclusive jail interview with a black radical. This black radical, who went by the name of Sandy X, was technically in jail for nonpayment of child support, but Jeffrey and the black radical agreed that the charge was transparently false and that Sandy X was actually in jail for being a black radical. Jeffrey's interview had been pretty inflammatory; I had a first-hand look at it because Jeffrey gave the tape to me to type. Both Jeffrey and Sandy X had used the term "bourgeoisie" a number of times, and I was not at all sure about the spelling but I figured nobody else would know either.

The article, headed "A Victim of the Bourgeoisie Speaks Out" should have created quite a stir, but it didn't appear to register with anyone except Mr. Thompson, who expressed consternation. "But the man is a notorious fraud," he said, sounding bewildered. I reported the fact to Jeffrey, along with Mr. Thompson's recommendation that the next time we planned to feature a black activist we should first run the idea past somebody black, but Jeffrey didn't seem all that concerned.

Then it turned out that we had at last attracted the attention of the official student newspaper. The faculty sponsor, Mrs. Venable, who was so old that she was referred to as Mrs. Vegetable, announced to her journalism class that it was a sad day when the staff of a radical underground newspaper knew how to spell "bourgeoisie," while some of her own students were still having trouble with "Lanier."

This recognition should have been good news, but it was about this time that Jeffrey ran afoul of Dave and Rick, both of whom cornered me in the hall to report excitedly that they had evidence that telepathy was real. "Huh?" I said.

It developed that during the course of a conversation about lunch, they had simultaneously stated, in unison, "Jeffrey is a dickhead." I felt that while this might constitute evidence of telepathy, it was more likely just a case of an idea whose time had come.

Dave and Rick were annoyed with Jeffrey for ignoring the Decency Rally phenomenon, which they felt was an affront to individual thought. These Decency Rallies were being held all over the country to encourage people not to behave indecently. I had gone to one at Cramton Bowl; it was notable only for the number of rednecks in the crowd. It was kind of like going to the fair without the entertainment value.

At least the paper had covered the Sesquicentennial. This event was held to commemorate the 150th anniversary of Alabama's founding, and featured in addition to a musical in which Patty Harris appeared along with 149 other people, a really weird exhibition of fountains. The spectacle took place in the Garrett Coliseum, a huge auditorium designed, for some unknown reason, to resemble a giant modernistic turtle. The Coliseum was the setting for the rodeo, the occasional rock concerts sponsored by WBAM, and all the state fair exhibits which didn't involve livestock. For the Sesquicentennial, the Coliseum's main floor had been rigged up with fountains which sprayed tall columns of water in a shifting pattern of colored lights. I didn't know what that had to do with being 150 years old, and neither did Dave and Rick, who had titled their article "All Wet," and had hinted darkly that someone in state government owned a controlling interest in the fountain business.

Meanwhile, Eddie and I decided that the *First Amendment* should tackle the issue of the midi-skirt. Having spent the best years of our lives trying to get around the administration's campaign against the mini-skirt, we were annoyed to discover that someone in the fashion world had apparently taken a bribe to make skirts longer. I had in fact circulated a petition against the midi-skirt, forwarding it to Belk's with the notation that none of the 74 people signing would be buying any midi-skirts so the store had better give up the whole idea of stocking them.

"Midi-skirts are a feminist issue," said Eddie firmly, pointing to an article in *Ms.* Eddie thought pretty much everything was a feminist issue, but I had to admit she had found an interesting article by Gloria Steinem, who in addition to pointing out that the fashion industry was dominated by men, said that women needed to exert control over institutions, including publications, which aimed to influence how they thought. She named *Ladies Home Journal* as a prime example. At some point recently it had occurred to the women who worked there that, while the magazine was named *Ladies Home Journal*, all the high paying reporting assignments went to men, while the women staffers were relegated to typing. The women had accordingly marched into the magazine's head office and gone on strike. Gloria Steinem thoroughly approved, noting that their next step should be tackling the magazine's popular feature "Can this Marriage be Saved" and renaming it "Hell No."

"We need to make sure we're getting bylines," added Eddie and I quite agreed. Even though the *First Amendment* didn't pay anything, there was still no point in being treated like suckers.

Before we could demand bylines, another controversy emerged, though this didn't directly involve the paper. The *North Tower* came out and we discovered that the school's literary magazine had been sabotaged. A story about doomed lovers was supposed to end with one lover surveying the aftermath of a fiery plane crash, clutching in his hand a piece of paper with the heartbreaking phrase, "PS I love you." Instead, somebody had altered the galley proofs so that the final sentence of the story now read "Inspected by No.13." The author was livid and so was Mrs. Vaughn, the magazine's faculty sponsor. An investigation was launched, but the culprit remained a mystery.

I was livid, too. The paper, which Jeffrey had just arbitrarily renamed the *Spectre*, must do something, I said indignantly. Jeffrey was inclined to blow me off, saying that I was "becoming obsessed with this thirteen business." Really, he should have been the first person to sympathize.

An article of his which referred to socialism as "the bugaboo of the middle class," had suffered a typo and appeared in the paper calling socialism "the bugaloo of the middle class." Most of our readers probably thought he was talking about the dance.

"And what about our bylines?" I demanded, with Eddie chiming in "Yeah!" Jeffrey was conciliatory, noting that Eddie and I would be listed on the masthead of the very next edition. "Well, we better be," we said menacingly.

A couple of days later, Eddie and I snatched up the next issue, hot off the mimeograph. Listed after Harold Jeffrey, Intrepid Editor, and Rick Smaltz and Dave Currens, Astute Intellectuals, were Kathie Farnell and Eddie Joyner, Nimble Fingered Typists.

In unison, Eddie and I said, "Jeffrey is a dickhead."

Only one question remained: what would Gloria Steinem do?

Graduation

Graduation was right around the corner. What was I going to wear? It was a sobering thought that at this point there was not much the school could do to you. The administration seemed to have figured that out. In the three years I had been there, it had issued strictures against short skirts, pantsuits, and halter tops (probably because with halter tops nobody wore a bra) and, recently, going barefooted. Now its instructions about how all 650 of us should behave at graduation had taken on something of a note of despair. The latest edict prohibited us from flipping the tassels on our mortarboards. It had become the custom for students to wear the tassel over their right eye going up to get the diploma, then triumphantly flip it to the left on the way back from the stage. This action seemed to enrage the administration, which had responded with the no-flipping rule.

You would have thought that at this point Lanier, and everybody else, had bigger things to worry about. At Kent State, which was in Ohio, the National Guard had opened up and killed four students, including at least a couple who were minding their own business. As far as I could figure out, Kent State had certain elements in common with the Boston Massacre. Both had involved soldiers firing into a crowd of civilians, some of whom had been throwing things. In Boston, the items thrown were rocks; at Kent State, the missiles included, according to one report, "a can of smoked fish."

Protests were held nationwide in reaction to the Kent State murders. At University of Alabama, a building was burned and the administration had ended the semester early and told everybody to go home. I was glad I wouldn't be going to Alabama in the fall.

At Lanier, things were somewhat lower key. A group of students wore black armbands to protest the shootings. Another group wore red, white, and blue armbands to express their opinion that Kent State had been asking for it. One morning before English got started, Debbie Brinker, head of the red, white, and blue squad, who up till now had been distinguished solely by a wardrobe consisting largely of ugly homemade dresses, accosted Francie and demanded to know why Francie was wearing a black armband. Unfortunately, Francie was having one of her inarticulate days. All she could manage was a mournful "wow, man," before the bell rang and we all went back to studying punctuation.

The school didn't issue an anti-armband ruling, probably figuring that we would all be out of there in a couple of weeks anyway.

Things were, I knew, going to change. Eddie Joyner and I had already quit the underground newspaper, following what the last issue had lamely referred to as "a clerical strike." That issue, filled with typos, was in fact the paper's last hurrah. It hadn't even gotten around to Kent State.

In fall, Eddie and I would be going to Montevallo along with Lizzie and Annette—all four of us had been impressed by the geode. I would of course be rooming with Annette. We would have the whole summer to plan our college careers, which were bound to be more interesting than our high school careers. The Diversified Office Occupations class was splitting up. Johnny Barber was going to Alabama; he wasn't scared, he said, because the building they burned didn't even have people in it. Nobody else in the class except me was going to college. They would keep working at the jobs they'd had all year or go to John Patterson Trade and Technical School.

A lot of them would be getting married, even Gladys, who had worked with me at Blount Brothers and who was getting married to someone she had met at church. The fact that Gladys would be leaving Blount Brothers to work in her husband's family hardware store had enabled me to make a lucrative career move. By some fast talking, I had arranged to work full time at Blount Brothers during the summer. This would give me time to stockpile money for college, since I would be pulling down a cool $50/week.

I planned to spend at least part of that money on a college wardrobe. I could start, I thought, with something sophisticated to wear to graduation. I expressed these thoughts to Annette, who was in the unenviable position of having to wear her Catholic High uniform to graduation. I told her she should wear whatever she liked, since the school wouldn't be able to do anything. She gave me a weary look which suggested that I hadn't been paying attention. Annette seemed a little subdued these days even when we talked about college, although I had picked out a couple of dynamite avocado green whipcord bedspreads which would add an undeniable note of class to our dorm room. That was another thing; we were going to be living in New Women's Dorm, which had private bathrooms. Who wouldn't be excited about that?

I figured Annette's lack of enthusiasm was due to some malign influence coming from Hal, who along with everybody else had been sent home from Alabama, which he portrayed as a seething hellhole, adding darkly that Montevallo was probably just as dangerous.

Though I tried my best to reassure her, the only time Annette really perked up was when we talked about Prom dresses. This Prom was not my first rodeo. I had gone to the Prom sophomore year with a weird blind date cooked up by Patty Harris' mother (and the fact that Patty had declined the honor should have tipped me off). Junior year I had grudgingly gone with Thor, and this year since I was temporarily between boyfriends I went with somebody random from algebra. Annette had of course gone with Hal, though she seemed more interested in the dress she had worn, which was pink and had an Empire waist.

Frankly, my Prom dress was a lot more sophisticated. I had gone to Belk's and bought a white eyelet dress which Mama had criticized on the grounds that it cost $40. Patty Harris wasn't sufficiently cosmopolitan to appreciate the dress either; it had a full skirt which she claimed made me look like a lampshade.

Ignoring Patty who was obviously jealous, I decided to customize the dress by making the skirt even fuller, thinking that my chic appearance would sound the death knell for the Empire waist. To ensure maximum volume, I would construct a nylon net petticoat.

You would think that in the capital city of a state you would be able to find white nylon net, but you couldn't. I had to settle for a petticoat made of green nylon net, which unfortunately sort of accentuated the whole lampshade motif.

The Prom was, I told myself firmly, a thing of the past. Meanwhile, as the date for my liberation from high school drew closer, I got an idea.

Skipping school.

Ray was always doing it, and so far had not been caught. There were just too many students; the principal couldn't be everywhere. I could skip the last day of class. I had passed all my courses and had purchased a yearbook and put a deposit on my cap and gown. The school was powerless to stop me. I had one problem; I still didn't drive and couldn't see myself going to the trouble of skipping in order to just roam around Sears all day. Fortunately, Francie was sympathetic to my predicament. We would all skip school, she announced, indicating me and Howard, a hippie she was now dating.

I felt a little uneasy at the prospect of getting in a car with either of them at the wheel, but on the other hand we were setting off first thing in the morning; not even Francie would be totally wasted at that hour.

As soon as Mama dropped me and Ray off, I slid out the side door of the school and met Francie and Howard in the parking lot. I didn't look to see if Ray actually headed for his first class, figuring it was none of my business.

Now the question was where to go, or as Francie put it "Where to, man?" Howard was devoid of suggestions; he was busy looking out the window and singing "Hey Jude." Fortunately, I had thought this through. We would go get donuts and then head for The Magic Mushroom Head Shop. Both Fairview Donuts and The Magic Mushroom were within walking distance of my house. If Francie and Howard started having acid flashbacks or whatever, I would just go home. Both my ideas were approved and we wobbled out of the parking lot, Francie talking encouragingly to her car, which apparently enjoyed interaction. We got a bag of donuts and one of donut holes; Howard became fascinated with trying to stick the holes back into the donuts. I just ate mine. By the time we convinced Howard that he should leave the donuts alone, The Magic Mushroom was open.

Located in an old house which had formerly been the site of the Lady B Lovely Beauty Salon, The Magic Mushroom still smelled like a home permanent, although the patchouli incense was helping. The guy in charge didn't even look particularly like a hippie; he drooped languidly behind the counter, talking on the phone to somebody about a party he had attended. "And I just decided to let my hair down," he was saying in a world-weary voice. I wasn't sure I wanted to know what this had involved. At least the guy didn't bother us. Francie and Howard looked at everything in the store, more than once in the case of some items. I was interested in the Indian shawls but settled on an incense burner and some incense for my future dorm room.

Then I realized it was nearly time for lunch and that I could walk home and eat my pimiento cheese in peace. The walk took me right past Cloverdale School. I didn't see Clay outside; he was either in class or had sneaked off to Bobby's house. Walking clarified my thinking. By the time I finished my sandwich, I had come up with the ideal fashion statement for my finale at Lanier.

At graduation, under my robe I wore the top half of a pantsuit. It was a halter top; the sort where you didn't wear a bra.

On the way back to my chair, I flipped my tassel.

Summer

The summer after I graduated, I got a taste of what it was like to work full-time.

I didn't like it. The main problem was having to get up early even though it was summer.

The actual job wasn't so bad. Blount Brothers Construction was located downtown in an old building which had a problem with damp; one day Mrs. Robinson found toadstools growing in the ladies room on the eighth floor. Mrs. Robinson was my boss. Annette said she wouldn't like working for a woman but, as I explained, that was crap. Mrs. Robinson was a good boss; she urged me to take my break even though I had pointed out that by working straight through I could easily finish the typing she had given me. I also liked her because frequently towards five p.m. she would say, "Time to fold up our tents like the Arabs, and silently sneak away."

One surprise about Blount Brothers was that I was now working with Dana Sue Oliver, whom I had known from Diversified Office Occupations class. Dana Sue had quit what she referred to as "the job from hell" at the hospital and had promptly been hired full time at Blount Brothers, which was suffering the loss of Gladys and Mary Susan to marriage. Dana Sue would also be getting married, she hastened to point out, but not till next year because her fiance was currently in Viet Nam.

Annette was sympathetic to Dana Sue's plight, and in fact seemed very interested in my job at Blount Brothers, asking a number of questions about my duties. Since they consisted solely of typing, filing and answering the phone, there was not a lot to tell. Anyway, thinking about my job didn't take up a lot of my leisure time.

That summer the main source of entertainment was Japanese monster movies, to which I went pretty frequently with Eddie, Dave, and Rick. We had a good deal in common, since we all hated Jeffrey, but our foursome wasn't destined to last. Eddie and I would be going to Montevallo in the fall, and Dave and Rick were headed to Alabama. Sometimes Lizzie came with us, but she seemed a little preoccupied. Ann had graduated from Auburn and had promptly taken off for

California with Frank; they hoped to become major players in the Farmworkers' Strike. Thanks to Ann, Lizzie would severely criticize anybody she saw eating grapes. I couldn't see Lizzie being very happy at Montevallo if she went around critiquing everybody's snacks. I was glad I would be rooming with Annette, who couldn't care less about grapes.

Annette still wasn't displaying the degree of enthusiasm I expected over our impending freshman year. She had agreed that avocado green cafe curtains would perfectly set off our avocado green bedspreads but that was pretty much as far as it got.

Unexpectedly, Dana Sue was proving to be pretty good company. Sometimes she joined me and Mama for lunch. We always met at the H.L. Green's lunch counter where Mama and I had vegetable soup with corn muffins and Dana Sue had a hot dog. Then we all had lemon icebox pie. After lunch if we had time Dana Sue and I would walk through Belk's where we would examine the pattern books and look at fabrics for my college wardrobe and her trousseau.

I had already settled on a pattern for a wool skirt and vest which I felt would strike a serious note, counterbalanced by the fact that the skirt was as short as humanly possible. Dana Sue, meanwhile, was planning a rainbow wedding; each of her many bridesmaids would wear an Empire-waisted polyester dress in a different pastel. I felt that moving past the universally- popular avocado color scheme was a bold decision on her part.

Even Annette perked up some when we decided to shop for shoes. We needed something which was both chic and substantial enough to prevent our falling down on Montevallo's uneven brick streets, while Dana Sue looked for shoes which could be dyed to match the bridesmaids' dresses.

I should have been having the time of my life, since I was earning money, picking out clothes, planning an exciting college debut, and going to monster movies, but there was a cloud over our household.

It was obvious that Ray and Clay were sliding further into what passed for the drug culture in Montgomery. They had apparently abandoned their marijuana farm, since Abicat continued in robust health, but my brothers were evidently finding plenty of pot somewhere. Oddly, I wasn't even tempted. Everybody I had seen stoned so far had behaved like a complete asshole. Although the same could be said for everybody I had seen drunk, I figured you didn't go to jail for being drunk unless you were driving a car, which I still didn't know how to do. It was fairly easy to divert people who passed me a joint by saying that I had bronchial asthma, which had once been true. If somebody showed up with brownies, I wasn't sure what I would do but figured I would think of something.

Viet Nam continued to occupy everyone's thoughts. The *Montgomery Advertiser* ran a feature on PFC David Winecoff, the son of our optometrist. According to the story, PFC Winecoff had narrowly escaped being killed in an ambush. He had then avoided capture by playing dead and reported that the worst moment of the whole incident occurred when a couple of the VC sat down on him to eat lunch. Viet Nam wouldn't impact our family immediately since my brothers were still too young. Besides, Ray was in no danger of being drafted because of his diabetes. Clay was another story. If the war continued, I could see him heading for Canada.

Meanwhile, he had given Mama some disquieting news. One evening, I got home fresh from viewing *Monster Zero*, which had as its premise an invasion from a planet where everything, including monsters, has a number. I felt this was a flawed concept and was still rather annoyed with the whole Japanese horror genre when I entered the house to find Mama visibly upset. Clay had gone to spend the night with Bobby, she said, after announcing that the coming school year would be his last. He was entering Lanier in the fall, but he would be dropping out as soon as he turned sixteen.

Frankly, I didn't really blame him.

Ray, who would be a junior in the fall, hadn't voiced any plans to quit school but Mama couldn't be sure that he wouldn't suddenly decide he had had enough education. This was, I knew, a blow. Both my parents had come from poor families and had worked to put themselves through college and law school. I tried to cheer Mama up by pointing out that my father's late brother Andy had left school at twelve and had still become a leading light with the Coca Cola company. I might have gone further and reminded her that Uncle Andy achieved his success despite a problem with substance abuse which had led him once while drunk to fall off the pier at Atlantic City, but I decided not to push it.

I was a little uncertain about leaving the family to go to college, but not uncertain enough to dim my enthusiasm for College Orientation, which was coming right up. I rode up to Montevallo with Lizzie, Eddie, and Annette in Lizzie's car. My Orientation roommate was a friendly girl named Annie Gruene, who said her last name was pronounced Green and that she was from a farm near Gulf Shores. I gave her a sympathetic look. My relatives in Mississippi lived on a farm; once their mule died and it was a big deal. Only later did I find out Annie's farm was a sizable ranch. It turned out that Annie sewed too, and in fact her dream was to open her own fabric store. She said she had selected Montevallo mainly because her older sister Doris was here majoring in business. I saw Doris once, from a distance. She was carrying a pile of books and looking vaguely harassed.

Annie and I meanwhile were having a good time. I thought guiltily that it was sort of a shame that I had already signed up to room with Annette, who was not enjoying Orientation that much. She complained that her roommate was a witch. This was literally true. The girl, whose name was Hilda, spent all her free time burning incense and muttering incantations, possibly designed to make Annette disappear.

The highlight of Orientation was our dorm tour. Annette and I would be living on the third floor of New Women's Dorm; our window overlooked a wooded area back of campus. It would be, I pointed out happily, the ideal situation, away from the hustle and bustle of Main Dorm yet plenty close to classes. Both Lizzie and Eddie were in Main; I wondered why they hadn't applied to room together but Eddie pointed out with some asperity that Lizzie was a Baptist while she personally was an Episcopalian and was not about to room with somebody who didn't drink. Nevertheless she seemed a little envious of Lizzie for having scored a room which shared a bathroom with the room next door while Eddie would be getting a room a considerable hike from the nearest toilet. While we were touring Main Dorm, an upperclassman came in, looking nonplussed. "Is there an Annette DeSalvo here? You have a phone call."

Annette looked suitably alarmed; she rushed down the hall to the phone booth, reappearing some time later to say, "It was Hal. He just wanted to make sure I was okay." Eddie rolled her eyes.

On the way home, we were all a little quiet. In less than a month I'd be saying farewell to my old way of life and the change might be something of a wrench. I would, I thought suddenly, even sort of miss Blount Brothers and Dana Sue. In an effort to cheer myself up, I turned to Annette. "We've got to make some decisions," I said happily. "Whose record player are we going to use?"

She just looked out the window.

Bad Roommates

Annette stood me up. I was notified at lunch. I had wondered why she wanted Mrs. DeSalvo to accompany us to Morrison's Cafeteria since I thought we were only going to discuss whose record player to take to Montevallo. I had just noticed that Annette didn't seem to be eating much when she came out with "Listen..."

It was, of course, thanks to Hal, who had finally convinced her that going to college was a serious mistake guaranteed to bring humiliation on her family when she inevitably flunked out.

"Right," I said. There wasn't anything I could do about it. Maybe, I thought, I would like my new roommate.

I saw her bedspread before I saw her. I had lugged my stuff, including the record player, avocado green bedspread and matching cafe curtains into the room and dumped them onto what I assumed was going to be my bed since it was the one without the lilac dotted-swiss bedspread with matching dust ruffle. At that point a perky brunette appeared and announced herself as Donna Jo Jutton, adding gratuitously that her last name was French, that she was from Georgia, and that she had been Miss Moultrie of 1969. She was, she confided, planning to major in music. By this time she had been on campus roughly two hours and had already informed the entire music department as well as several bystanders that she had been Miss Moultrie, so when people started referring to her behind her back as Miss Poultry, I felt a sort of grim satisfaction.

A couple of days later I sought out Annie Gruene. "Jutton," I said, "isn't French. Jutton is redneck."

Annie nodded gloomily. We were sitting in her dorm room at the time, and she pointed out that her situation was in fact worse than mine. She had been supposed to room with Helen Broome from home, she said, but Helen had decamped with the heir apparent of the family which owned The Hub Tub, a popular laundromat, just one week before school started. "And she had picked out the bedspreads," Annie finished, indicating the bed upon which we were sitting.

Snoopy.

I had to admit that was worse. Just then Annie's roommate blew in. Her name was Teresa, she went by Terry, and she was swinging a softball bat. She said something that sounded like "Argh," and bounced back out. "PE major," said Annie.

Eddie was in much the same boat. Her roommate in Main Dorm, also a PE major, was named Roberta, went by Bert, and insisted on calling Eddie "Ed." I wondered if Bert knew Terry.

I saw Lizzie in the cafeteria and she was also gloomy. I didn't know why, since she had a room on the first floor with an adjoining bathroom. It turned out that she also had a roommate who was confined to a wheelchair. "She didn't even mention it," said Lizzie angrily, apparently referring to an introductory note from Claire, the roommate. I wasn't sure what to reply, since "maybe she thought you wouldn't notice," was obviously the wrong response.

It seemed to me that Lizzie still had it good compared to the rest of us. She had a room on the first floor, and if she had to share a bathroom, at least she wasn't sharing it with Miss Poultry, whose monogrammed towels were all over the floor.

The roommate situation was dismal, but in many ways, life at Montevallo was less fraught than life at Lanier. Montevallo might as well have been trapped in amber, or Jello, since the 1950s. There was not only no violence on campus, there was not much of anything on campus. There were only a few hippies, and there certainly wasn't going to be any racial upheaval at Montevallo, since by my count there were only three black students. One of these, Roz Hollins, was in geology with me and immediately won my admiration by identifying a ferruginous rock as "one of those ferocious rocks."

Montevallo was not exactly a party school. Once classes were over for the week, everyone who could, left. There were more girls than guys among the students, and girls who had hometown boyfriends were grimly hanging on to them. I began to feel I had been shortsighted in cutting my Montgomery social ties, such as they were.

Meanwhile the outside world continued its downhill slide. In the first six weeks of school, both Jimi Hendrix and Janis Joplin died of drug overdoses. I was going home to Montgomery every weekend, and when I got there I was almost afraid to ask what was new. Ray and Clay weren't able to do much to commemorate the brief life of Janis Joplin, but they had a full complement of Jimi Hendrix albums, and "All Along the Watchtower," played at top volume, reverberated through the house nonstop.

Meanwhile, Mama had a date.

I was mildly nonplussed. Mama had just turned fifty and was still a dazzling brunette. Since my father's death, however, her social life had consisted largely of taking care of me, my brothers, Granny, Abicat, and her string of elderly freeloaders.

Now she was going with somebody random to the world premiere of *The Traveling Executioner*, a movie which had been filmed entirely in Montgomery at Kilby Prison. Kilby no longer housed prisoners but was apparently still atmospheric, especially the former Death Row. I wondered what would happen if Mama actually liked this guy, and figured her best option would be to run off with him. Abicat could come live with me and Miss Poultry, and the cops would undoubtedly see to it that Ray and Clay had a secure place to stay for the next five to seven years.

Once I got back to school, I awaited Mama's account of the date with bated breath, but other than reporting excitedly that she and her escort had gone to the Elite Cafe where they had ordered, according to her, Brandy and Benzedrine, she didn't say much about it. She must not have thought getting back in the swing of things was worthwhile since I didn't hear any more about the guy.

Other than Mama's date the big news at home was that Annette had snagged my job at Blount Brothers. Okay, I didn't want it, but still. I had stayed friends with Annette partly out of inertia, and it was rather awkward listening to her prattle on about Dana Sue's wedding plans while knowing that upon my return to campus I would face Miss Poultry and her musical friends. These pals of hers had the bad habit of congregating outside the back door of the dorm and bellowing "Donna Jo" up three stories until Donna Jo finished hot rolling her hair or whatever and leaned out the window to see what was up. Sadly, she never leaned out far enough.

During all this hoopla I was sustained by my courses, which were really pretty interesting. I was able to stay in contact with the campus geode since I was taking geology, but I wasn't sure what my eventual major would be. It was still expected that I would go to law school, and I was still unenthusiastic about the prospect.

Meanwhile, we were all finding out that Montevallo had a number of traditions. Freshmen were supposed to wear a sort of beanie thing, which we didn't. Then there was Senior March. The seniors were supposed to select a night on which they would pounce upon the unsuspecting underclassmen, dragging them into the basement and, according to one report, pelting them with grits.

"Right," I had said, and had then devoted considerable energy to making the dorm room senior-proof. The ideal outcome would have been if Donna Jo had been, say, out in the hall when the college chimes began playing the "Dead March," the signal for the attack. In that case, I could have just nonchalantly locked the door. Instead, we were both in the room and as the first notes sounded I, as we had practiced, vaulted over to the door and locked it, after which we both hid in the bathroom. Nobody on our hall got captured; the housemother was appalled at our lack of school spirit.

Time slowly passed. Eventually I realized that the end of the semester was coming, and that it would bring changes. "I'm leaving," said Annie one November day. She had had enough, she stated, of people calling her Annie Greensprings. I didn't blame her since the popular wine was reported to contain formaldehyde. Annie was going home to start her own fabric shop.

Lizzie was leaving, too. She would be transferring to Alabama. I pointed out that Alabama still had violence on campus, and Lizzie said grimly that she would take her chances. Eddie had gloomily decided to continue to room with Bert, who was out playing basketball most of the time anyway.

Meanwhile, Miss Poultry had developed two hobbies: belching and cracking her knuckles. Since she was taking voice, I supposed belching could be something they assigned her to do, like practicing scales, but I wasn't sure about the knuckles. As the last straw, she began practicing for the Christmas chorale. "Fa la la la la la la la la la," she trilled.

I'm out of here, I thought. I would apply to move to Main Dorm. No bathroom, but no Poultry.

No-brainer.

I was able to go home for the holidays as soon as my geology final was over, catching a ride with Lizzie, who was equally uninterested in attending the Christmas chorale. She had big news: Ann and Frank had been married by a Moonie.

I agreed that that was cool. Talking of getting married reminded me of Dana Sue, who by this time was surely in the home stretch with her wedding plans, and this in turn reminded me of Annette. I would, I decided, call her as soon as I got home.

I had expected Annette to be filled with Christmas cheer and probably planning her own rainbow wedding. However, she was obviously steeped in gloom. What was it? Hadn't she heard from Hal?

She had.

Hal was getting married, to somebody he had met at Alabama.

Science Fiction

One reason that Montevallo was boring was because it had apparently been founded as some sort of rural reform school for girls. To discourage escapees, the campus had been located in the middle of nowhere miles from the nearest rail line; in an emergency you probably could have gotten away by stealing a horse. At a certain point the school had become a college and eventually it had gone coed, but nobody much noticed. When I arrived, there seemed to be about seven girls to every boy, and this interfered with my original plan to boost my social life.

Computer dating.

This scheme, which had looked foolproof when I was still in Montgomery, involved me setting up a computer dating service. The idea was, all these boys and girls would fill out applications, and I would fix myself up with the top 10% of the guys. I would also charge everybody $5. The main problem with this plan was not the fact that I didn't have a computer. I had explained away that detail by telling everybody that the computer was too large to fit in the car so they should just pay the $5 and fill out an index card, which I would enter in the computer when I returned to Montgomery for the weekend. Right away, people balked at paying $5, so I had to drop the price to $1. Then I noticed that the only people signing up were girls. I finally had to tell people that the computer was in the shop and I didn't know when it would be fixed.

When I figured out that Montevallo was in the throes of a terminal shortage of boys, I decided that the best option was to join a sorority, since they seemed to have gotten the inside track to what few guys there were. There weren't any sorority or fraternity houses on campus. The sororities had their own hall in the dorm, where the members led lives of unimaginable luxury replete with amenities including, as I noticed on the one occasion I visited, a pinup of Olympic swimmer Mark Spitz.

Unfortunately, immediately before going out for Rush, I had written an article for the student newspaper in which I referred to sorority members as "a gaggle of overdressed parasites," and it turned out some of them had read it.

Finally, I hit upon the ideal solution for improving my social life. I started a Science Fiction Club.

It was true that the science fiction club I had visited at South Alabama was a bust, but surely that just reflected bad management. I felt certain that with me in charge things would be different.

Starting the club was a breeze. I just put a notice on the bulletin board at the Student Union Building inviting people to sign up. I had recently gone to the Swiss Colony deli in Birmingham where I had impulsively bought a carton of clam dip, which it turned out I didn't like. Now, I saw that it would come in handy. The poster announced that at the first club meeting "Clam Dip will be Served."

That'll get them, I thought triumphantly.

Sure enough, despite the fact that the signup sheet contained a number of obvious fake names, Ray Bradbury being the most popular, quite a few people turned out for the first meeting and the clam dip was an undeniable hit. I was a little startled when it turned out that Lyn and Betty, the other two girls who had shown up, were majoring in home ec, since I didn't think home ec majors were interested in reading anything which didn't mention vanilla extract. It developed that Lyn, despite being the mousy type, had caught the fancy of an even mousier guy named Henry, who was a big fan of *Star Trek*. Lyn's roommate Betty, a chunky live wire, had apparently come for the clam dip, though it turned out that she and Lyn were both fans of the television show *Dark Shadows*. Of the guys present, Wayne and Norman were amateur cartoonists and Barry, a zoology major who had a pet snake, liked the Fantastic Four and claimed he could get us a faculty sponsor.

Dr. Harvey, a mild-mannered biologist, seemed interested in being our sponsor, indicating conspiratorially that he had access to a mimeograph machine. I didn't know what good that was supposed to do us, but it turned out to be handy for publicizing club projects, like the Science Fiction Club Short Story Writing Contest, which was a great idea since it was guaranteed that we would always win our own prize.

Our meetings tended to settle into a routine. We would talk about which movies we would plan to see if somebody ever got a car, then we would talk about *Star Trek* reruns which were on every afternoon, and then we would eat the refreshments that Lyn and Betty had brought. These refreshments were pretty much a mixed bag; their quality depended on which food group Lyn and Betty happened to be studying that week. The unit on turnips was a bust.

I thought we were getting into a rut with these meetings and it was time to shake things up, so when spring came and the weather improved, I organized a club picnic to the campus lake.

This was a success, since Lyn and Betty had baked a cake, but otherwise all we really did was eat sandwiches and throw rocks in the water.

Something's got to give, I thought, and sure enough right after that Wayne's older brother got a better car and sold Wayne his old one, and somebody showed up at the club meeting with a notice about the Science Fiction Mardi Gras. This event was going to be held in a hotel in downtown Atlanta, and a whole lot of science fiction celebrities had been invited, including Isaac Asimov. I was a little worried about the fact that they didn't say that any of the celebrities were actually coming, but everyone in the club agreed that it was something we should check out.

I already had a plan for coming up with money for the trip. There was a large sign in the campus book store: "We Pay Cash for Books!" and it wasn't as if I couldn't borrow somebody else's textbook if I needed to. Furthermore, I already had a great outfit for the Costume Contest—I still had my silver paper dress from high school. I planned to say I was a Rigellian, since nobody knew what that was supposed to look like.

Wayne's brother's car turned out to be big enough for our whole contingent, although somebody had to sit on the floor. Barry wasn't going; he was worried about Clyde, his snake. "I don't like to leave him with a sitter," he said, and I said I understood perfectly.

When we got to downtown Atlanta, I was excited to see the Regency Hyatt, which was topped with a restaurant which allegedly revolved. We had a really good look at the Regency since Wayne got lost and went past it three times. Eventually we figured out that our hotel was some blocks away in a rather sketchy section of Atlanta. We could hear a lot of sirens as we got our bags out of the car, and when we checked in the desk clerk said we should be careful and not leave the hotel after dark for any reason. I didn't think this would be a problem since we would probably have all the excitement we could stand right there at the Mardi Gras.

The hotel was so old that the rooms still had kitchenettes. Norman was overjoyed; he was always trying to save money and in fact had brought his own food. This sounded like a good idea until it turned out that his food consisted of several cans of green beans. He had also brought a Jiffy Pop, but it didn't inflate like it was supposed to because the stove had a defective burner. I wasn't worried about food since I was rooming with Lyn and Betty and the home ec department had finally finished studying cruciferous vegetables. Lyn had also generously supplied food for Henry, who was rooming with Norman and Wayne.

It turned out that the Science Fiction Mardi Gras was pretty disorganized and consisted largely of weirdly-dressed people wandering around asking where the celebrities were. Our costumes were a hit, though. Norman and Wayne were both dressed as robots; they had used up a couple of cartons of aluminum foil in the process. Henry and Lyn, thanks to Lyn's sewing prowess, were *Star Trek* crew members, and Betty had come as a Martian belly dancer. Apparently she had not paid attention during the diet and nutrition unit that semester; there were several remarks to the effect that she had plenty of ammo. I didn't win a prize for the Rigellian outfit, but at least it hadn't cost anything, and a guy who was dressed as a squid asked to take a picture of me.

Finally we bumped into somebody who had brought two cases of homemade beer, and we spent most of the evening riding up and down in the elevators. The trip was, I thought, an unqualified success.

On the way home, Wayne and Henry took turns driving, since they were the only ones with licenses, and we all compared notes. Wayne and Norman were thrilled that they had gotten to meet the cartoonist who drew Silver Surfer, Henry and Lyn had made friends with another couple dressed like *Star Trek*, and Betty had given her address to an abominable snowman who promised to write.

I was happy that I now had an exciting social life and had gotten to see downtown Atlanta.

Besides that, I would be back in Montevallo in time to watch *Star Trek.*

Mrs. Abernathy

Sometime during spring semester of 1971, I realized that English was turning out to be my favorite subject thanks to Mrs. Abernathy, who was incredibly sophisticated. She had white hair, even though she was only in her forties. She spent every summer in Europe and had all her clothes made by a dressmaker in Birmingham. She lived in Thorsby on a farm with her husband Hank, who taught in the math department, yet she radiated urbanity.

I might have been destined to admire Mrs. Abernathy from afar if I hadn't started coughing. I was living by this time in Main Dorm with a roommate named Jane who was not as obnoxious as Poultry, though she was secretary-treasurer of the Baptist Student Union. When I started coughing I assumed it would go away. Then it didn't. Mrs. Abernathy stopped me as I was leaving class one afternoon. "You're coughing," she observed. "Are you taking echinacea?"

I wasn't taking anything, but didn't see how echinacea, whatever that was, would hurt. Echinacea turned out to be a tea, my cough went away, and Mrs. Abernathy became my mentor. She knew about all the latest important ideas, like echinacea. She wore Earth Shoes, which I had no intention of wearing because of the way they looked, but I still appreciated her initiative in buying them.

Mrs. Abernathy was the perfect antidote to my other teachers as well as the people I was interacting with at my job. At the start of spring semester, I had begun working part-time at the Alumni Office. My job consisted of opening the mail, during which I wound up reading a disheartening lot of communications which began "Please take me off your mailing list as I have no intention..."

I depended on English class to cheer me up.

Eddie sat behind me in class, and one day we were thrilled to be invited to Mrs. Abernathy's for dinner. That was another interesting thing about Mrs. Abernathy. Although she lived on a farm fifteen miles from campus, she maintained an apartment in an old building right across the street from the science building. The apartment was decorated in global style with everything Mrs. Abernathy had amassed in her travels and in fact reminded me of her office, which boasted several tombstone rubbings she had done herself.

On the night of the dinner party, I was frankly feeling a little overdressed, since I had chosen to appear in a formal with a crepe skirt and velvet top which I had bought at an after-Christmas sale for $35. Everybody else had on jeans except for Mrs. Abernathy, who had on a silk dress. I stood and watched her, fascinated, as she added wine to a saucepan full of English peas, something I had never heard of anyone doing.

"I only wish Susan Whitworth could have been here," she said meditatively. "The two of you would hit it off, I'm sure."

Mrs. Abernathy seemed devoted to the mysterious Susan Whitworth, who got mentioned a lot. She sounded even more sophisticated than Mrs. Abernathy since she had been with the Birmingham Ballet until, as Mrs. Abernathy said, it became obvious that her real interests lay elsewhere. Susan Whitworth traveled to Europe every summer with Mrs. Abernathy and had apparently done so for years.

I was fascinated by Susan Whitworth. I figured she was a college professor whose work kept her away from Montevallo. Since she was an ex-ballerina, maybe she was a patron of the arts. In fact, she might be a philanthropist. I was looking forward to meeting her if Mrs. Abernathy ever remembered to introduce me.

That was the thing. Mrs. Abernathy was forgetful. Sometimes she wouldn't show up for class. Once she forgot to show up for an exam, though we had to take it later anyway. Occasionally she seemed to forget where I was from, since once she began commiserating with me over being from "one of those horrible little Black Belt towns." I felt that the capital of the state, a city with more than 100,000 people, probably shouldn't be referred to as a little town. Montgomery was in the Black Belt, though, and I reserved judgment on the horrible part.

I was in fact headed to Montgomery right after this conversation and for a change I was going there for something interesting.

Mama had written a book. She had begun writing poetry right after Granny died, her creative impulses having been pretty well stifled before that. She had shown me her poems back when I was working on the *North Tower* and asked rather diffidently whether I thought she ought to have them published. I agreed enthusiastically, especially after she pointed out that if she published a book she would include one of my poems. Her book was entitled *Dappled Sunshine* to acknowledge that her life had included both light and shadow. In fact, Mama had had a very difficult life and it would have been more accurate to name the book *Black Clouds*, though I didn't think it would have helped sales.

One of her best poems was about her friend Mary Liles, who had died right after my father. In the poem, Mama wrote about visiting her terminally-ill friend in the hospital, and neither one of them being able to talk about anything but shoes. Mama liked writing about nature, but her later poems were darker and included several about Viet Nam. I thought she was probably worrying about my brothers.

Clay had been as good as his word, bailing out of Lanier the minute he turned sixteen. He was currently working as a deliveryman for an auto parts store and had more or less moved in with an older girl named Louise who had an apartment in an old house downtown. Ray was still in school, but his hair was longer than mine and he spent all his free time hanging around The Magic Mushroom with a group which Mama referred to as hooligans. The upside was that the house was only half as noisy since we just had Ray playing records full blast, though "Sympathy for the Devil" had now joined "All Along the Watchtower" as the official background music.

My trip to Montgomery was partly to attend Mama's book signing at a shop in Normandale Shopping Center and partly to get a copy of *Dappled Sunshine* to take to Mrs. Abernathy. Mama happily inscribed the book "to Kathie's favorite teacher."

Mrs. Abernathy was very complimentary and said that she intended to show the book to Susan Whitworth. "I keep telling her she needs to write a book about the Birmingham Ballet," she added. I said this was a great idea and that Susan Whitworth probably had a lot of interesting insights.

As the semester rolled on, I began thinking that I should major in English. I had been toying with the idea of majoring in business like Annie Gruene's sister Doris, but finally had been forced to conclude that I already knew how to type and was getting more than enough clerical work to last me at the Alumni Office.

In fact, I was thinking seriously about quitting my part-time job. Mrs. Abernathy was completely opposed to the idea of me stifling my creativity by working at the Alumni Office, and I couldn't have agreed more. "Why don't you run for newspaper editor?" she asked. "You had experience in high school." She was probably referring to my poem from the *North Tower*, not my experience with the underground newspaper, but I felt she'd had a good idea so I promptly gave notice at the Alumni Office and signed up as a candidate.

I was elected newspaper editor partly as a result of Mrs. Abernathy's enthusiastic backing and partly because the person running against me was widely known as a dipshit. I was overjoyed with the results, though. I would be making $300 a year, while garnering all sorts of prestige.

Meanwhile, one day in class Mrs. Abernathy announced we were going to see a special slide show featuring her Summer in Europe program, open to everyone, which involved earning class credits while touring England and the Continent. Halfway through the show, Eddie poked me. "We're going," she said. This made sense. Eddie and I had become friends. We were planning to room together in the fall, Eddie having gotten disenchanted with her roommate Bert the PE major, who, she said darkly, had gotten the wrong idea just because Eddie was called Eddie. She would also, she said, be glad to get off that particular hall since it had been plagued for a couple of months earlier in the year by an obscene phone caller and as the hall's only committed feminist she had been frequently required to settle the guy's hash. Meanwhile, I was pretty fed up with Jane, who was not at all shy about giving her testimony.

When I told Mrs. Abernathy I wanted to sign up for Summer in Europe, she was enthusiastic. "Wonderful! Come to my office at four— you'll get to meet Susan Whitworth. She just got back from New York. She'll be going with us this summer."

I was overwhelmed.

When I arrived at Mrs. Abernathy's office five minutes early, I was mildly surprised to see a kid there. Since she was obviously too young to be in college, I figured she was looking for her older sibling. When she saw me, she smiled broadly.

"Hi," she said. "I'm Susan Whitworth."

She was Susan Whitworth Abernathy, Mrs. Abernathy's daughter, and she had just turned fifteen.

Tricky Dick Strikes Again

I spent the summer of 1971 in Europe and came away with two insights: I was destined for a career in television; and Richard M. Nixon was a crook. It took me longer to figure out the second one.

Eddie and I had traveled to England together and we met the rest of the group a couple of days before classes were to start. In addition to me and Eddie, the group consisted of Susan Whitworth, two guys named Don Hammond and Wilson Couch who appeared to have crushes on Susan Whitworth, a girl named Lucy Beth Gilroy who was one year older than Susan Whitworth and who may have been mistakenly seen as a steadying influence, and Marty Holbeck, known as a relatively harmless nerd. I noticed during the introductions that Eddie seemed to be eyeing Marty suspiciously. "Your voice is familiar," she finally said.

That's when it all came out. Marty, rattled, confessed to being the obscene dorm caller from back in the spring. He claimed, not very believably, to have been forced into it by the bigger guys on the hall. "Why'd you quit?" asked Eddie. "Were you about to get caught?"

"No," said Marty. He shuddered fastidiously. "There was this awful, terrible girl who would get on the phone and say these—" he looked at Eddie suspiciously. "Your voice is familiar," he said.

Next to Marty, the oddest person in the group was probably Lucy Beth, who like Susan Whitworth was from Thorsby but who lacked Susan Whitworth's patina. Her family, she reported, had a lot of money and in fact she had been assigned to buy as many clocks as possible while she was in Europe because her mother was thinking of opening a clock shop, which Thorsby lacked. Her family had been disappointed in the accuracy of her passport photo, which her father felt hadn't captured the real her, and had arranged to have Lucy Beth professionally photographed. She passed around the passport, which showed her hair as a good deal blonder along with other evidence of heavy retouching. It also showed a considerably slimmer version of Lucy Beth, who sighed in acknowledgment. "I suffer from bloat," she confided. After she left to get an ice cream, Mrs. Abernathy spoke up. "Lucy Beth isn't bloated," she stated firmly. "Lucy Beth is fat."

We were a motley crew, but we settled into a routine soon enough.

We were all taking two courses: English Literature, taught by Mrs. Abernathy; and Fundamentals of Broadcasting, taught by a variety of British teachers. All classes were at the University of London's Richmond branch which was quite a hike from the dorm. For English Literature we would spend every weekend roaming around Stratford on Avon or Canterbury or some other literary place. The television classes, meanwhile, included a number of interesting behind-the-scenes insights including the fact that in England you could get away with anything by showing up at a person's door with a clipboard and announcing "I'm with the BBC." I made a note.

It had been two years since I had last been in London and the main thing that had changed was the number of hippies. London was inundated with them. They clumped on the steps of all major buildings including the British Museum. At least there weren't many around the dorm.

Meanwhile, as the summer progressed, it became obvious that Lucy Beth was not a steadying influence on Susan Whitworth, whose sophistication couldn't alter the fact that she was jailbait. Often it fell to me to drag her out of harm's way while Lucy Beth only seemed interested in whether some of the guys deflected from Susan Whitworth would fall to her lot. I wasn't exactly sure of the logistics, but it seemed to me that Susan Whitworth was attracting all this attention because she had long red hair and because she had an unnecessarily-extravagant figure. It was possible her admirers didn't realize she was underage. Then again it was possible they did.

When I wasn't seeing the sights or babysitting Susan Whitworth I was answering my mail from home. Mama was a little evasive about how Ray and Clay were doing, but at least Abicat was still in good health and the book was selling well. In response, I sent air letters which usually described whatever cultural experience I had enjoyed that day along with observations on how it could be improved. For one thing, although I was a big fan of afternoon tea, I didn't understand why I couldn't get it iced.

Finally classes ended and we headed for the Continent for the final two weeks of our trip. Mrs. Abernathy had arranged to buy a Volvo from the factory and pick it up dockside in Calais. She was the first person I had ever heard of doing such a thing. We wound up packing me, Susan Whitworth, Lucy Beth, and Eddie in the car. Marty was going to stay in England and visit relatives. Don and Wilson were going off on their own although they were hampered by an imperfect grasp of European geography. They had already suffered one misadventure, boarding what was advertised as the plane for Copenhagen only to find themselves, after a lengthy interval, in Moscow. Mrs. Abernathy said hopefully that we would see them at the Rome airport.

Our trip through France was enlivened by the fact that we had to pretend to be Canadians to avoid violence from French citizens upset by the war in Viet Nam. This ruse worked like a charm since our accents were obviously not American. The only downside was that people kept asking us for Canadian cigarettes.

Meanwhile, the car was getting fuller and fuller due to everyone but me buying stuff. Lucy Beth had at least a dozen clocks and Mrs. Abernathy and Susan Whitworth had bought a lot of cashmere sweaters. Eddie had bought boots. The only thing I had gotten was a scarf in the Ferguson pattern for Mama.

I noticed something disquieting as we puttered through the French countryside in search of cathedrals. I had assumed that since Lucy Beth was obviously a moron, Eddie and I would spend the whole trip making fun of her. Now, however, Eddie was hanging around with Lucy Beth and the two of them seemed increasingly inclined to make fun of me.

It was, I decided, jealousy. I had appointed myself navigator, since Mrs. Abernathy's grasp of the configuration of Europe wasn't much better than than of Don and Wilson. In fact, she sometimes seemed unsure of what country we were in. Being the official navigator meant that I had to sit in front and increasingly there were complaints about crowding from the back seat along with unfair criticism of my navigating.

Then came Limoges. We were staying in a faintly sinister rooming house with a toilet which seemed haunted since it had a habit of suddenly flushing by itself. One morning Mrs. Abernathy, who had gone out to secure some rolls for our breakfast, came back in something of a panic. "We've got to get out of here!" she blurted. "It's Nixon!" I was worried that he had landed troops at Dunkirk, but it turned out to be sneakier than that.

Nixon had devalued the dollar.

While no big deal to anybody who wasn't in France with most of their dwindling funds still in dollars, the news was a major blow to us. We had enough francs to pay our rooming house bill and to gas up the Volvo, but that was about it. We had to get to Switzerland, since through some technicality which I didn't grasp we could get our money changed there at a favorable rate.

Switzerland! Where was Switzerland? I pulled all the maps out of the glove compartment, ignoring the remarks from the backseat.

Our best bet, I announced, would be to head cross-country for Geneva. This was easier said than done. For one thing, the roads were not all that well-marked and once or twice we found ourselves on what might have been a game trail. For another thing, Mrs. Abernathy wasn't completely familiar with how her new Volvo worked and on one occasion, trying desperately to reverse out of the way of a large truck, she succeeded only in turning on the windshield wipers.

Tempers ran short, especially on the part of Lucy Beth, who was holding what looked like a heavy mantelpiece clock on her lap and complaining every time it struck the hour.

Only Susan Whitworth remained unruffled. She had been traveling with Mrs. Abernathy since childhood so she had pretty much seen it all. At her suggestion we stopped at gas stations for food since we had enough francs to get snacks which Mrs. Abernathy purchased as I shooed French gas station attendants away from Susan Whitworth while Eddie and Lucy Beth made unhelpful remarks.

The sun had set and Lucy Beth's clock was striking nine as we bounced over the border into Switzerland, where the border guards took their usual long time ogling Lucy Beth's passport photo and Susan Whitworth in person before ushering us in.

We were not out of the woods yet. It was obviously not going to be possible to stop Lucy Beth from purchasing at least one cuckoo clock. Furthermore I was now harboring doubts as to whether Eddie and I were really cut out to be roommates.

However, Nixon had been foiled, our finances were secure, and as soon as the stores opened I was going to buy myself some Swiss chocolate.

Frasority

My roommate was a jerk. Eddie had been exhibiting symptoms while we were in Europe but it was not until fall semester started that she really burst into bloom. She developed the habit of greeting everything I said, no matter how hilarious, with "Christ." She managed to say "Christ," which she pronounced as "CHRiiiiist," through her nose, adding a note of sophistication.

To make matters worse, we were both supposed to be working on the *Alabamian*, where I was the editor and Eddie the circulation manager until she either quit or I fired her depending on who you asked. My prestigious position as editor was turning out to be a lot of work, especially now that I had to lug all the papers around campus myself. I was also taking a lot of heat for some of my fighting editorials, particularly if I happened to call somebody a Nazi.

Amid all this brouhaha, I was happy to have a visit from Annette, who thought Eddie was a jerk, too. Arriving on a Friday in her new red Vega, Annette had been full of tales from her new job with Calhoun Construction. It was, she said, a step up from Blount Brothers. In fact, she worked in the Calhoun Office Park, which she referred to as Headquarters, and though she had only been there a short time she had been entrusted with the keys to the entire facility. She brandished an enormous keychain equipped with a doorknob to keep her from losing it in her purse. The thing must have weighed ten pounds, and I doubted she could have lost it in her house. Not only that, said Annette happily, but Mr. Calhoun Jr. had done her the honor of putting her name down as the person to receive a telephone call should the burglar or fire alarm get tripped in the middle of the night.

We were having this conversation in my happily-empty dorm room, Eddie having favored Annette with a look before ostentatiously departing.

"I don't see how you stand it here," Annette said, surveying the room fastidiously. She had brought a can of Raid with her, since she was deathly afraid of roaches, and now she issued a surreptitious squirt in the direction of Eddie's closet. In fact, Annette was so worried about roaches that she slept that night on my desk. I thought about pointing out that roaches could climb on a desk with little more effort than they expended in climbing on a bed, but I figured it wouldn't do any good. Annette had some odd habits when it came to sleeping. The one time I spent the night with her in high school, I hadn't gotten much sleep, due to the fact that she had the mattresses on her twin beds hermetically sealed in some sort of extra-crackly plastic. She also had a nightlight, since she couldn't sleep if it was dark, and the radio was on since she couldn't sleep if it was quiet. I thought the dorm room would probably strike her as too dark, too quiet, and too roachful, and I was right.

The following morning when she announced that she was going back to Montgomery early, I had suddenly said "I'll go with you."

Mama, though surprised, was overjoyed and announced we would have pizza. She would pick one up, she said, on her way back from dropping Ray off at Sharon's. Ray had a girlfriend. Her father was in the Air Force and she looked like a peroxided version of Sonny Bono, but Ray seemed besotted with her and Mama was constantly in demand to chauffeur him to and from Maxwell Air Force Base.

Clay had lost his job at the auto parts place but was still living with Louise. Mama was worried about them. "They spend all their time over at that Mike Moran's," she confided. Mike Moran lived over by the new Mall and apparently had his own room over the garage at the house he had shared with his mother and her second husband until, according to Mama, Mike's bad behavior had broken up the marriage. Mike had now become something of a local drug celebrity; over the summer I had heard a radio DJ dedicate a heavy-metal song to "all the heads at Moran's psychotic room."

Meanwhile, since I was in Montgomery for the weekend, I spent some time with Annette. As far as boyfriends went, she was at a temporary loose end since she hadn't managed to replace Hal right away, but, she said brightly when she picked me up, she had some exciting news. "I've started a Frasority," she reported.

"Huh?" I said.

Once we got to her house, she explained fully. "Frasority," she said, sitting herself on the bed, which crackled alarmingly. "It's like a cross between a fraternity and a sorority. For people who didn't go to college. Now they can have as much fun as people who did." Having as much fun as people who went to Montevallo wasn't going to strain anybody, but I was a little curious about the concept. Annette said she hadn't thought it up; somebody she worked with had a cousin in Macon, Georgia, who belonged to one and had sent her the details. Apparently, membership in a Frasority didn't require anyone to move out of their parents' house, go through Rush, or have weird initiation ceremonies. Instead, you got together with your fellow members twice a month, drank beer and made crafts.

"Huh?" I said. At this, Annette scrambled through a drawer and came out with an odd-looking necklace. "I want you to have this," she said generously. "I made it out of paper clips." The paper clips had been covered with avocado green Contact paper. "The girls all made one," she continued. "The boys made these." From the shelf over her bed, which ordinarily held a music box topped with a ballerina, she retrieved a lopsided goblet. "See? You just get a glass-cutting kit, cut the base off a wine bottle, turn it upside down and cement the base to the neck." It looked like it would hold a lot of wine.

The Frasority wasn't meeting that weekend, so Annette suggested we go out and have drinks at a club. I wasn't sure how we were going to do that. We had fake IDs and hers was even laminated, but the problem was that at the time I left Montgomery there were no actual clubs. There was a bar at the bowling alley called Kegler's Kove and a fairly disreputable place called the Embers on the Atlanta Highway, and you could get a drink at restaurants, but otherwise if you didn't belong to the Country Club you were pretty much out of luck.

Apparently I hadn't kept up with events, though, because Annette pointed out that Montgomery now had an actual bar called Coaches Corner, over by the Mall. "I go there a lot after work," she said happily. Coaches Corner was located in a strip mall next to the eye clinic. The sign featured a confused-looking guy in a referee's uniform juggling a basketball, baseball and football. The sports motif continued on the inside; the walls featured posters for Alabama and Auburn football. There were quite a few people in the bar, and several of them asked me if I taught school. Annette surveyed the surroundings and suddenly brightened. "It's Mister Honeycutt!" she breathed. This Honeycutt turned out to be a squat, bulbous guy with a very red face who plowed his way over to us. "I'm Mister Honeycutt," he stated. "Do you teach school?" "I'm Ms. Farnell," I said, since he was being formal, "And no." Everybody laughed. Annette explained prettily that Mister Honeycutt's first name was actually Mister, since he had been the first boy born in his mother's family since roughly 1870. He was president, she added proudly, of Honeycutt Asphalt, a name which was familiar to me from a newspaper article titled "Wallace Cronies Strike it Rich." "Kathie's visiting from college," continued Annette.

"Alabama or Auburn?" asked Mister.

I couldn't fault Mister for his generosity; he bought me a Singapore Sling and Annette a CC and Seven-Up (which, she had told him confidentially, was Her Drink), but he seemed rather creepy in addition to being old enough to be Annette's uncle. I was sort of relieved when the entertainment started, but instead of a band they had an odd-looking bald guy dragging a big case. "This guy's great," said Mister happily.

The guy, who was billed as Baldo and Billy, kicked things off by stating that his act had been called "a little too sophisticated for Montgomery." While he was saying this he brought out a can of spray paint and sprayed his head gold. I sat up, unsure if he remembered what had happened to that woman in *Goldfinger*. He didn't spray anything other than his head, though, before opening the case. "And this," he announced, "is Billy!" Billy was a very big snake which Baldo then draped around his shoulders. That was pretty much it. He didn't paint the snake gold or try to juggle him or anything. Nevertheless, his act may have been a little too sophisticated for Annette, who said she felt faint, so we left.

When Annette called me on Monday, she seemed enthusiastic about something, but quieted down immediately when I told her I was going back to Montevallo. "Mama's going to drive me."

"Oh," said Annette. "Are you sure? You know, if you came back to Montgomery I could get you a good job. Mister was very impressed. He's looking for a secretary. I'd take the job myself if I didn't have all these responsibilities. I'd just hate to let Mr. Calhoun Jr. down."

On the way back to Montevallo, I thought. I would have to come up with enough money to get a room by myself. The problem was partly Eddie, who was a jerk, and partly that I was not cut out to have roommates. I was already editor of the newspaper, which paid a little, but I could get another job too. As Annette had been quick to point out to Mister, I could type.

Meanwhile, Eddie and I would just have to learn to live together. How hard could it be?

I waved goodbye to Mama and pulled my suitcase into the dorm, where I was immediately met with Eddie. "Christ," we both said.

Hippies

The end of 1971 was uncharacteristically peaceful. In Montgomery I got the latest from Annette (who was still auditioning new boyfriends) and Patty Harris (a freshman at Alabama, she was being insufferable about pledging a sorority). I heard about Lizzie and Francie by going out in a desultory fashion with Francie's brother Thor, who reported that Lizzie liked Alabama and that Francie was in California living with a radar operator. I wondered if Francie had reformed; a stoned radar operator would be a dicey proposition.

I also saw Miss Bonnie, Mama's best friend, who brought her daughter Lana to lunch. I had been afraid of Lana as a child, even though she was a little younger than me, because she had belligerent red hair and liked to jump on people. She still had red hair but was now confining her belligerence to being a committed feminist activist at Vanderbilt. She was wearing army fatigues, scowled a lot and upbraided Miss Bonnie for not leaving a big enough tip, saying that she was oppressing the masses and was in danger of becoming a tool of the patriarchy.

I didn't get why Lana was so mad. After all, the Equal Rights Amendment was going to be passed any minute and after that we'd have equal rights and get paid the same thing as men and everything would be great, unless you believed the people who said we'd have to use the same bathroom.

Later, Mama confided that Miss Bonnie was worried about Lana. "She thinks Lana has fallen in with hippies," said Mama. "I wish you'd go up and visit her. You could be a good influence."

I doubted that Lana was interested in being influenced, but as it happened I got an invitation to Vanderbilt just at the time I needed a break.

I was having trouble managing being editor of the *Alabamian* on top of my class overload, which now included courses in television and radio. I was still rooming with Eddie, who was giving me the silent treatment (which frankly was better than when she talked). The situation was temporary—Eddie had announced through an interpreter that she was transferring to Huntingdon at the end of the year and my job as newspaper editor would run out at the same time.

Meanwhile things were grim. Then they got worse.

I had a phone call from Mama. Abicat was dead.

He was nine, in his sixties by cat reckoning, and his kidneys had suddenly failed.

I took to my bunk and refused nourishment, not that anybody offered me any.

Just a couple of days later, though, I got a call from Lana, who had apparently been put up to it by Miss Bonnie. Would I come up to Vanderbilt for a visit?

I arrived by train. Lana, who was driving a friend's van, greeted me effusively and toured me around campus, saying we would get hamburgers and then go to a sneak preview of a new movie, *The French Connection*. We agreed later that it was the stupidest movie we had ever seen and that nobody would pay to see a bunch of car chases and people getting shot.

The next day we had lunch with hippies. Patty and Bill were a little unusual, said Lana, since they were married and Bill's mother lived with them. They were living in an authentic hippie house, though; everything was tie dyed except the macrame plant hangers. Bill worked as a carpenter, said Lana, Bill's mother Jean worked at the post office, and Patty apparently sat around eating. I had to admit that I liked Patty's outfit. It ran heavily to gypsy, incorporated significant Navajo influence and was topped off with a velvet cape which might have come from some down-and-out opera company.

When Jean served lunch, I was happy to see an entire table full of food I hadn't had much of since the death of Granny, who had done our cooking. There were bowls of collards, sweet potatoes, and blackeyed peas. I dug in. Patty seemed downhearted that her own cooking didn't measure up. "Don't you worry, honey," said Jean. "First time I got married I was fifteen and couldn't cook nothing but cornbread."

The cornbread was excellent. Bill, who had actually grown the collards, showed us around his backyard garden, complete with chickens. "We just get their eggs, man," he explained hurriedly. "We don't kill them or nothing." I said I was sure the chickens appreciated it.

Since these were hippies, I figured there would be dope involved and sure enough as we were leaving Lana entered into a muffled consultation with Patty, who produced a baggie from under the couch. "This is for an experiment," said Lana conspiratorially.

I had noticed that Lana's dorm hall featured a number of posted notices of which "No Tie Dying in the Washers!!!" sounded the most exasperated. These were the work of Betty, the dorm adviser, who was felt to be a killjoy, and it turned out the experiment consisted of getting Betty stoned. The contents of the baggie were mixed with a plate of spaghetti intended for Betty. "Sorry there's not enough to go around," said a girl named Bernice apologetically. "It's okay," I said.

When Betty dug into her personal serving, she looked a little surprised. "What's that unusual flavor?"

"Oregano," said everybody. Betty nodded. "It's actually very good," she said condescendingly. She finished eating, stared into space for a minute, uttered an odd laugh, and went to sleep with her head in the plate.

With Betty out for the count, things livened up. Somebody produced a number of bottles of Boone's Farm and at least one of Night Train. The more Lana drank, the more belligerent she got. All the doors in the dorm had wooden ventilator slats near floor level, and Lana decided to take out her feelings about the patriarchy by kicking them in with her hiking boots. "Take that!" she yelled. "Calm down, man," said Bernice, indicating Betty, who was still passed out but had now fallen from her chair.

Once she calmed down, Lana became morose. "Wow, man," she said. "This is terrible, man. I can't stop saying 'man,' man." She was about to kick in another ventilator when somebody announced that they were going to burn a zilch.

I was a little alarmed, but it turned out a zilch was a plastic dry cleaning bag tied in knots. It was suspended over a wastebasket full of water, the lights were turned out, and the bag was set on fire.

It dripped impressive blue flames into the water, making a noise which, while it wasn't exactly "zilch," wasn't anything else either. Then Bernice produced a box of Tide and sprinkled it liberally on the floor and somebody else turned on a black light. The results were impressive, just like walking on the stars, man, as somebody said right before Lana kicked the wastebasket over.

The next morning found Betty locked in her room, answering all entreaties to open the door with a worried "they're coming to get me!"

Lana, somewhat the worse for wear, surprised me by saying we were going to Folk Mass. This was odd since Miss Bonnie was a Presbyterian and Don, Lana's father, was usually too hung over to go to church, but Lana was very enthusiastic about Father Larry. He was not a bit patriarchal, she said.

Folk Mass took place in a storefront just down the street from campus. The parishioners were a motley crew and included students as well as people who looked as if they had recently escaped from an asylum. We sat on folding chairs and Father Larry kicked things off by welcoming all us folks to God's living room before delivering his homily. "Everybody's doing the best he or she can, man."

Sad but true, I thought.

Father Larry looked sort of like a Muppet, and when he pulled out a banjo I thought for a minute he was going to sing "It Isn't Easy Being Green," but he swung into "Let My People Go," adding a couple of lively banjo riffs. I figured he was doing his best.

Then he launched into a prayer for all victims of a number of varieties of oppression, including lynching, unfair employment practices, light pollution (here he mentioned astronomers), deficit financing, the sales of over-caffeinated diet drinks, and littering.

I was hoping we could leave when he finally ran out of oppressors, but instead he invited everybody to come to the Tuesday night Hootenanny and then it was time for Holy Communion. This involved the grownups surging forward to get wine and crackers and all the kiddies, who had up until then been running around screaming and yelling, surging forward to get punch and Oreos so they wouldn't feel left out. Lana beamed. The wine wasn't bad.

As we were finally allowed to trickle out, Larry produced the banjo again and urged us to join in a rousing chorus of "Go Tell It on the Mountain." He reached the part about "who's that yonder dressed in black," everyone but me yodeled "must be the hypocrite turning back," and I realized I had on a black coat. They couldn't possibly have aimed the song at me, but I still said "assholes," though not very loud.

The next time I went to Montgomery, I reported to Miss Bonnie. Was Lana surrounded by hippies? "Don't worry about hippies," I said reassuringly. "There's a lot worse things."

George's Ghost

My friend George Williams died in early 1972, right after Abicat. Mama had met George over the summer while I was in Europe. In fact, she had met him in the laundromat. While waiting for her clothes to dry, she had thought of something funny and had started laughing. George had immediately thought she was cool so he followed her into the drugstore.

At that time, George was nearly thirty and had been back from Viet Nam for five years but he hadn't ever gotten over it. He had been wounded in combat and had subsequently gotten hooked on pain pills. In spite of, or because of, his drug problem, Ray and Clay immediately became big fans of his; Mama liked him for his sense of humor and because she felt sorry for him.

George was the first hippie I actually liked, and he was a trip. He hated driving so whenever he had to go anywhere he always drove at top speed to get it over with. At one point he became convinced that the Chinese were going to conquer the earth so he learned Mandarin through the Berlitz program.

I had last seen George just before Christmas. Back in the fall, he had embarked on another adventure, enrolling in Auburn University with the intent to major in international studies. He thought his experience would give him an edge since he already spoke Mandarin and had visited a foreign country, even though it was Viet Nam. He was, though, a little worried about his grades. Mama counseled him to think of what else he might like to do in case college didn't work out. "Nope," he said. "If this doesn't work, that's it."

One week after grades came out, he shot himself.

None of us really recovered from George's death. We couldn't go to his funeral; since he was a suicide, his family didn't have one. Ray and Clay brooded. They both already had their troubles. Ray was getting ready to graduate from high school and Sharon was getting ready to break up with him since her family was being transferred to Germany. Clay was still with Louise but they were having what Mama referred to as "non-marital trouble" so he was around the house a good bit. The music was still loud but had a gloomy overtone made worse by the fact that a lot of it was by Jimi Hendrix who was dead.

I was busier than ever with the *Alabamian,* and even though Eddie would be leaving soon, living in the dorm was getting all over my nerves. To make my job as editor even more impossible, I was on closed study hours and was supposed to be in my room studying between seven and ten p.m. I was nearly caught a couple of times while in someone's room transacting newspaper business. Once I had to hide in a closet and once I nearly went down the fire escape slide, deterred at the last minute by the fact that I was on the third floor and by the fact that the fire escape slide looked scary.

At this point I had some good news from Mrs. Abernathy. I had told her about George and she had commiserated that it was really bad karma. Then a few days later she came out with the welcome announcement that she would like me to work in the English department starting in fall.

Meanwhile, in a few months I would be leaving the paper, but not the world of publishing. I had been elected editor of the *Tower,* the campus literary magazine. It didn't pay as much as the paper, but every little bit helped since I was going to summer school and would be paying for a private room.

The Science Fiction Club continued its successful run, but big changes were coming. Henry, Lyn, and Betty were graduating. Lyn and Henry were getting married in the fall and Betty had surprised everyone by running off at Christmas with the guy she had met at the Atlanta Science Fiction Mardi Gras. She was, she announced, secretly married. I thought she should stop telling people if it was a secret. Barry, meanwhile, had suffered a heartache. Tina, his girlfriend, had run off with Earl, his roommate. Barry's only consolation was his snake, Clyde. "It's just the two of us," he said sadly.

Partly to cheer him up, the Science Fiction Club started showing old movies in the English department classroom after dark, charging fifty cents admission. Norman was able to rent these movies by mail. Even after paying the rental and postage, we made a tidy profit which we invested in snacks.

In my last month at the paper, George Wallace was shot. There wasn't anything the *Alabamian* could do about it but run an editorial about gun violence. I worried that the shooting would usher in a wave of rioting like what we'd had in the Sixties, but things quieted down before classes ended.

I was in Montgomery long enough to see Ray graduate from Lanier and immediately go into a tailspin at his girlfriend's desertion, and then I went back to Montevallo. Mama came out of the Main Dorm room which was supposed to be my own to report "you have a roommate but she seems nice." This was the equivalent of telling someone "you have termites but they seem nice." I informed the girl, who did seem nice if slightly perplexed, that I was supposed to have a private room. Then I packed up my laundry basket and left. Once I finally got the room I had paid for, I was able to customize it, taping paper over the air vent to block the sub-zero air conditioning, and putting place mats on one of the desks to show it was reserved for dining.

Then I had to find a place to hide the vodka. I had acquired a bottle of cherry vodka which tasted a lot like cough syrup, but mixed with Coke it wasn't bad. It was necessary to conceal it because dorm counselors had a bad habit of searching people's rooms.

After a little thought I had come up with the ideal hiding place. I stood on a chair next to the wall and pushed up the dropped ceiling panel. Then I leaned over and put the vodka on top of the ceiling of the room next door.

This vodka was actually part of an important experiment. In addition to my television courses, which I felt I would ace, and bowling, in which I planned to win the "most improved" prize, I was taking chemistry. Since I was having trouble with the periodic table, I had developed a scientific method of studying. I theorized that if I got drunk and studied, then got the same degree of drunk and took the test, I would have clear access to the information since it would be on the same wavelength. I could see this discovery revolutionizing education, kind of like Montessori.

While I was developing my theory, I got a letter from Lyn, who was working away on her wedding plans. Since she had lived with Betty the whole time she was in college, she seemed fairly nonplussed at my news that I didn't have a roommate. She also seemed worried about me being "all by yourself."

Unfortunately, that wasn't the case.

I first noticed George while sitting under the water tower eating a hamburger. I didn't exactly see him but George was there, sort of hovering. I noticed him the same way I had noticed Granny. I thought it a little odd that George, who had never been to Montevallo, should be haunting its water tower but unfortunately a few days later I noticed him in the dorm room.

I wondered if this had something to do with Cambodia. One of George's worst memories from Viet Nam was about having to ambush a bunch of Cambodians, an action which particularly bothered him because he had liked Cambodians and in fact wanted to be reincarnated as a Cambodian.

Had Cambodia rejected his application?

I tried talking to him. "What's up, George?"

I was even able to give him some good news. The US and Vietnamese had stopped arguing over the shape of their conference table and were now actually negotiating a peace agreement which might see troops being pulled out of Viet Nam by the end of the year. "See?" I said. "You don't have to hang around here. Everything's going to be okay."

He never said anything, and in fact never appeared, but he was still there.

Then he started showing up in the bathroom.

It was bad enough to have to go down the hall in the middle of the night to the bathroom, without somebody hovering invisibly in there. It was a very sad thing, I thought, if George, who in life had been cool, had to spend all eternity being a pervert.

I thought long and hard. Maybe George was brooding because he didn't get to have a funeral. At that point, I called Annette. After some desultory conversation in which I noticed that she had started referring to her boss Mr. Calhoun Jr. as "Ricky" I asked her about having Masses said.

Yes, she said, you could have a Mass said for somebody who was already dead and she didn't think it was illegal to have one said for a suicide, though she couldn't swear it would do any good.

I promptly called the Catholic church, which was within easy walking distance of campus, and made an appointment. I didn't say anything about George being a suicide, since I wanted to be sure the priest gave the Mass his best effort. I sealed the deal with a hefty donation.

It was money well spent.

I didn't notice George after that.

I hoped he would like Cambodia.

Streakers

My experiment in studying while drunk had not gone as well as it might have. I decided I had failed to allow for daily changes in my metabolic rate; to achieve optimum results, I would have to get drunk and study at the exact time of day as the exam. As the fall semester of my junior year arrived, I reluctantly chalked the whole thing up to experience.

Things had settled down a little. I was now living in New Women's Dorm—by myself, and with my own bathroom. To top things off, I was no longer editor of the *Alabamian*. Mrs. Abernathy had come through with her offer of a job in the English department. Part of my work involved tracking Mrs. Abernathy down on occasions when she had forgotten she was supposed to show up on campus to teach a class or administer an exam. Locating her could be tricky; she ranged all over the county going to estate sales and once I was compelled to drag her out of an auction in Pelham just as she was bidding on a piano.

I sometimes had to enlist Susan Whitworth to assist me, but finding her was a little tricky too. She was currently preparing to spend her spring semester in England and was otherwise preoccupied with fighting off the long-distance attentions of a sheikh who, she confided, was perfectly capable of having her kidnapped and added to his household. I had to admit that Susan Whitworth's problems were a lot more interesting than mine.

Meanwhile, even though I was no longer the editor, I still covered stories for the *Alabamian*, and was also kept busy advising Muffy Freely, the paper's new editor. Running a newspaper, I informed her, had its pitfalls; I was still dealing with the fallout from last year when I had completely forgotten that Montevallo had a basketball team. As far as editorializing went, I counseled her not to shy away from controversy. She was currently unsure whether to print an editorial response to the continuing allegations involving Richard Nixon and something cryptic that had happened at Democratic headquarters. I urged her to go for it, citing as an example of crusading journalism my own editorial response to a campus-wide shortage of toilet paper earlier in the year. I felt that my editorial, headlined "What Do They Want Us to Do,

Just Sit There?" had helped end the crisis. I further advised her that eventually the paper would have to take an editorial stance about one of the year's most controversial phenomena.

Streaking.

When I first heard about streaking, I didn't think it would catch on at Montevallo. A place that won't let you go in the dorm lobby without shoes isn't going to just sit there and let you run around naked.

Besides that, streaking was supposed to be a form of protest, and protest movements weren't exactly big at Montevallo. There had been two protests in the last year, one about the toilet paper shortage and one about the food in the cafeteria, but you couldn't call either one ideological. Nobody was sure what streaking was supposed to protest, but everybody agreed it was political. Some reporters thought it was a protest against the war, or about taxes, while others said it was a comment on free expression.

Ladies Home Journal said it was about free love. *The Atlantic Monthly* said it was a form of religious protest with roots dating back to Lady Godiva. *Ms.* called it an expression of anti-feminism. This was worrying, since anti-feminism would probably be very popular at Montevallo.

During the summer, I had noticed the phenomenon creeping closer and closer. Notre Dame had a Streakers' Olympics. Then people started streaking ball games. A bar called Streak McNasty's opened in Montgomery. The fact that it was in an old gas station sort of diminished its cultural importance, but still.

Finally, one day Mama and I were talking to Miss Bonnie, who was enthusing about the full moon of a few days earlier. "I could have streaked so easily," she mused.

This was, I thought, getting serious. If the proletariat adopted streaking, it wouldn't be a political act anymore, and would undoubtedly spread to Montevallo. Besides that, the proletariat would probably screw it up. Look what they'd done to long hair.

Sure enough, when fall semester started, streaking was already a topic of conversation on campus. I wasn't sure how things worked in other places, but apparently at Montevallo streaking was going to operate on a schedule. The news would spread that somebody was going to streak at a certain time and place, and everybody would turn out. Sort of like a parade.

One evening a group of us were standing around the college bell tower when Marty Holbeck sidled up and inquired what people were doing there. "Well," said somebody, "there was a rumor a guy was going to streak at 7, but it's already 7:10 so..." He was cut short by Marty, who wailed "my watch has stopped," threw aside his raincoat and streaked off in the general direction of the library.

Weirdly, the college didn't try to do anything about it. It's possible they were remembering about the fire drill. At a certain point, someone had noticed that although the girls' dorms had fire drills every time we turned around, nobody was making the boys' dorm participate. There were mutterings about calling the state fire marshal. Somebody wrote a letter to the *Alabamian*. Obviously, we weren't worried about the boys burning up; the feeling was that if girls had to get rousted out in the middle of the night so did boys. Finally the dean's office caved. They didn't think it would be a good idea to have an unexpected fire drill, though, so the date and time of the boys' dorm fire drill was announced—just like streaking.

Once the boys adjusted to the idea, they were behind it one hundred percent. The First Annual Fire Drill Party was organized, and the entire dorm spent the hours before the drill getting as drunk as possible. When the fire alarm sounded, all the boys tied their sheets together and jumped out the windows. One guy broke his arm. After that, the whole boys' dorm fire drill business quieted down; literally, since somebody got annoyed with the fire bell and pulled it out of the wall.

Once streaking hit campus, there were a number of incidents leading up to one memorable fall afternoon. At that time, a couple of the students were heavily involved in Living History military reenactments. From what I observed, this involved a group of people, mostly guys, dressing up like they were in the Revolutionary War and marching around, occasionally firing muskets loaded with noisy yet harmless black powder. After that they would camp out in Revolutionary War type tents, eat stew and argue about whose buttons weren't authentic. Eventually it would rain and they would go home.

This fall, their routine was interrupted by Bob England, the new membership chairman, who had a great idea. Why not arrange an historical reenactment event right on campus, on what would be the football field if Montevallo ever had a football team? The field, which an optimistic college official had even equipped with goalposts, presently served only as a parade ground for ROTC, but they weren't using it nonstop.

So one cool yet sunny day, the local chapter of Living History showed up in full gear, shouldered their muskets and marched in perfect unison up and down the field, occasionally presenting arms. A crowd gathered, some of the members wondering aloud when ROTC had gotten new uniforms. Bob was probably overjoyed, though in fact half the people present were there to see Marty Holbeck, whose career as a streaker had taken off since his appearance at the bell tower. He had now become a sort of unofficial college mascot and could be counted on to enliven any outdoor event.

I was there to cover the occasion for the *Alabamian*. As I had explained to Muffy, the paper had to keep up with campus events. I was prepared to spin the story either way. If Marty didn't appear, I would title the article "To Arms!" If Marty did show up, I would call it "Losing Streak" since I didn't like Marty.

Marty arrived just as things were reaching a crescendo. All the Revolutionary War soldiers had halted, lined up and aimed their muskets to deliver a rousing 21-gun salute. Right on cue, Marty scuttled in from the sidelines. A cheer went up, which the reenactors probably assumed was for them.

Then, three things happened. Marty turned to wave at his adoring public. The head reenactor yelled "Fire!" And Marty ran straight into the goalpost and fell flat.

"He's dead!" wailed a number of people. "It's another Kent State!" Two or three guys went to help Marty, who was groggily sitting up. The rest of the crowd was busy yelling "End the war!" or running away, except for a couple of guys who were asking Bob England how they could join up.

My article, headed "A Plea for Sanity," referred to streaking as a valuable means of commentary about free expression, war, religion, and pollution. I made up the part about pollution. At any rate, streaking was back to being political, and that's the last time it happened at Montevallo.

Lyn's Wedding

Lyn's actual name was Cora Lyn. She had dropped the Cora when she got to Montevallo on the grounds that it sounded like an old maid. This was a wise decision. By the time she met Henry, Lyn was about twenty minutes away from being officially certified as an old maid by President Nixon.

Both Henry and Lyn looked sort of spinsterish. In fact, they resembled the couple in the painting "American Gothic," except that Henry was shorter than the guy with the pitchfork.

Lyn and Henry were already engaged when I met them courtesy of the Science Fiction Club and for her upcoming fall wedding I was going to be the only attendant since Betty had decamped and was now living in Newnan, Georgia, and using address labels which gave her name as Mrs. Marcel Nutter.

There were an awful lot of people getting married. Annie Gruen, my friend from Orientation, sent a note saying that she had married Doug Fields and inviting me to visit Annie's Cloth Barn, her new fabric store.

The weirdest bride was probably Cissy Pitts, sister of Richie Pitts whom I had had the misfortune of dating in tenth grade. Cissy had always styled herself as a hippie and now it turned out she was marrying another hippie named Willie Mott, who looked like Charles Manson and who asked me, on the only occasion I met him, whether I believed in human sacrifice. That was one wedding I wouldn't be attending.

I had run into the happy couple in Montgomery where I was helping Lyn pick out material for my bridesmaid dress. I noticed as we combed through bolts of fabric that she wasn't giddy with anticipation though she did point out that since Henry had been commissioned a lieutenant in the Air Force, she would be an officer's lady. I thought this would make sense if she happened to be Jane Austen, but she wasn't. Lyn had had mixed feelings all along about marrying Henry, who was genuinely besotted with her. Once she had even broken up with him, but after he got drunk, wrote a poem about being drunk, and presented it to her, she had made up with him, probably worried that the next thing he handed her would be his ear.

I had a date with Thor while I was in Montgomery and told him that there was a good chance that Lyn was only marrying Henry because the alternative was being an old maid home ec teacher in what Mrs. Abernathy liked to refer to as "one of those horrible little Black Belt towns."

"So?" shrugged Thor.

I reported the incident to Mama, who responded "Strike him off the list."

Mama's list of suitors had been longer than some telephone books and she had spent a significant portion of her youth moving names from the Suitors list to the ever-lengthening Rejected Suitors list. I should, I thought, get a list. To save time, I would skip the Suitors tabulation and go straight to the Rejected category.

So far, I could list Thor, Richie Pitts, and Norman from the Science Fiction Club. In the midst of the brouhaha over Lyn's wedding, he had said that he and I should tell people we were engaged, then we would split up and divide the wedding presents. I had rejected the idea out of concern that he would renege either on dividing the presents or on not getting married.

Whenever I came down for the weekend, I noticed that the house in Montgomery was a good bit quieter these days. Ray was at University of South Alabama, still mourning the departed Sharon, though he had joined an organization calling itself the Roach-a-matics which spent its time getting stoned and going to Dauphin Island. Mama said grimly that if Ray's grades didn't improve he was headed for Auburn University at Montgomery in the spring. Clay, meanwhile, had gotten a job as a printer with the *Montgomery Advertiser* and was back living with Louise. He had also gotten a car, a 1961 Ford which had a serious defect: it would only drive in reverse.

He had backed over to see us a couple of times, though his main interest seemed to be Dingbat, an ill-natured black cat who had shown up on Mama's front porch during the summer. Clay had named him and probably would have taken him to live with him and Louise if Dingbat had not had the bad habit of biting people. He had already ambushed me and taken a plug out of my leg, and when Miss Bonnie had leaned over to speak to him, he had fastened onto her nose.

I was careful to keep Dingbat out of the way of people who called, especially if the person was giving me a ride somewhere. I would, I decided, have to give learning to drive top priority. Since I was trying not to rely completely on Mama, I had been reduced to soliciting rides from Annette, who was full of stories about her boss, Ricky, and his unhappy marriage, and even Patty Harris, who was in a sorority, dating frat boys and, she said, looking at jade engagement rings.

I informed her that there was no such thing as a jade engagement ring but she still had me worried, since I wouldn't put it past her to get married just to spite me.

One Saturday I needed to get to Montgomery Mall to look at trim for my bridesmaid dress, and I wasn't about to go with Patty on the grounds that the Mall had jewelry stores and I wasn't looking at any jade rings.

Fortunately I had met a random Air Force guy named Bill Hamner who had asked me to dinner and was willing to detour by the Mall. It developed that he was not happy that I was participating in a wedding since he seemed to have a jaundiced view of marriage. He said I was an enabler.

"On the list," I muttered.

Abandoning my social life, I decided to concentrate on sewing. Happily, Lyn had rejected the whole avocado green motif—my dress was a candlelight crepe chosen for its contrast with Lyn's stark white. By the time I went back to Montevallo it was finished except for the trim.

I was still living in New Women's dorm, but thinking seriously that I ought to be moving off campus. The main problem was food. At mealtimes I could eat in the cafeteria (which was always a bad idea), try to cook something in a popcorn popper, or muscle my way into the dorm's only kitchen.

This kitchen was destined to play a vital role in the completion of my bridesmaid dress, which was supposed to feature a frill of wide beige lace. Montgomery Fair didn't have any beige lace. I had had to settle for white lace. Then I had an idea.

I was happily boiling the lace in a pot with tea bags when somebody walked into the kitchen with obvious designs on the stove. She fled when I fished the lace, now solidly beige, out with tongs.

My dress finished, I could concentrate on the complicated logistics of getting to and from the wedding. Mama picked me up for the trip to Montgomery and I traveled to Union Springs, site of the ceremony, with Lyn's family. Henry, who was already stationed in California, would be flying in at the last minute. Their honeymoon would consist of driving back across the country pulling a U Haul. I promised to come visit them in La Jolla.

Lyn still seemed somewhat downcast, though she perked up a little just before we got to the Methodist Church. "In a way," she said thoughtfully, "I guess I'm lucky." During the ceremony, her resolve seemed to fail her; at one point I noticed that she was shaking so hard her bouquet was rattling.

The reception was held back at her parents' house and featured ham sandwiches and potato chips along with punch which, I was happy to see, did not contain lime sherbet.

There weren't many guests, but one old classmate of Lyn's from high school had shown up. Her name was Barb, she taught third grade in Opelika, and for some reason she had shown up wearing a suit. I looked around to see if she'd brought a briefcase. Barb decided to make something of a spectacle of herself. After pointing out that she was concentrating on her career rather than getting married like Lyn and everybody else from their class, Barb happily presented Lyn with a sketch pad, "because I want you to keep up with your art." I thought her concern was a little misplaced, since Lyn was only getting married, not being sent to Devil's Island.

Finally the happy couple left on their honeymoon, Lyn shooting me a final brave glance before the Oldsmobile swallowed her up, and I rode back to Montgomery with Lyn's brother, whom I immediately added to the Rejected Suitors list just in case.

My bridesmaid duties behind me, I settled back into the Montevallo routine. One afternoon the following week, I was headed to my job in the English department when I stopped off at the Student Union Building's bookstore. There on the magazine rack was the new *Bride's*. It featured a spectacular dress, a heavy cream-colored satin worn by a redhead who was actually laughing. This was the first happy bride I had ever seen.

The magazine cost $3.95. I was already late for work.

I bought it anyway.

Driving

After Lyn took off on her honeymoon, the only excitement left was the presidential election. Nixon was favored over McGovern, especially since the Paris peace talks had at long last borne fruit and it looked like the war might actually end. In fact, Nixon won by a landslide despite all those weird newspaper articles about him wanting to burglarize the Democrats.

Meanwhile, I still couldn't drive.

This was, I thought, getting ridiculous. Not only was I tired of being dependent on Mama or whoever I could talk into giving me a ride, I already had a car. Granny had not put in an appearance in quite some time, but she hadn't been idle because from the afterlife she had arranged for me to find her bankbook. When I started grade school, she had added my name to her savings account and at the time I found the bankbook in a kitchen drawer, it had a couple of thousand dollars in it.

More than enough to buy the 1968 Satellite Mama had seen in the paper.

Although the car's mechanical defects together with its green paint job would eventually lead to its being christened The Lime, it was still in working order when Mama and I happily puttered up to Montevallo, followed by Miss Bonnie in Mama's car. On the way up, I delivered what I assumed was good news. My television courses had been going well and in fact I had been offered a job at the campus television station upon graduation. I thought this was swell, but Mama fell silent when I told her. Finally she spoke. "I'm just afraid that if you stay in Montevallo you'll be an old maid."

This bloodcurdling prediction didn't make a whole lot of sense; I was just twenty and was adding to my Rejected Suitors list practically every time I met someone. I figured Mama was thinking of Carol Claiborne.

Carol was editor of the *Montgomery Advertiser Sunday Magazine* and Mama and I had met her earlier in the year when I did a freelance article for her about the campus geode. I wasn't sure how old Carol was but she was at least in her forties—plenty old enough to be an official old maid. She lived with her mother, talked in a high squeaky voice and, when startled, said "My Gravy!" Her worst habit was freezing food and then telling you how old the entree was while you were trying to eat it. The only other person I had ever known who did this was Patty Harris' mother, which said it all. Ray summed up the situation: "Carol is a dingbat." Worryingly, I had no idea whether the fact that Carol was a nut was the cause or effect of her being an old maid.

After Mama dropped me off at Montevallo and rode home with Miss Bonnie, I had several things to brood about. I had to pass my driving test and I had to come up with a career plan which did not involve being an old maid.

My alternative to a television career was law school, which I was resisting. I broached my dilemma to Mrs. Abernathy one afternoon in the English department while I was helping her look for her marriage license. "You aren't cut out for law school," she said. I couldn't hear her very well because I was currently wedged under a desk where she thought she might have dropped her license. "You're the creative type, like Susan Whitworth."

Susan Whitworth was obviously not going to be an old maid, since she wasn't even seventeen yet and was already fending off indecent proposals from sheiks. I was having to help her pack for England in addition to my usual duties and I figured once Susan Whitworth got there she would end up married to Prince Charles or somebody.

Susan Whitworth, continued Mrs. Abernathy, was going to be doing an internship with the BBC over the following summer. "You need to look beyond Montevallo," she said firmly. I agreed totally. At this point, Mrs. Abernathy remembered that her marriage license had been last seen in her husband's truck and the conversation about my future was put on hold.

The reference to me being the creative type reminded me that I had something else to worry about: "The Ginkgo Tree." This was a story submitted to the *Tower*. It was sure to be controversial since it concerned a gay guy who discovers that his boyfriend is cheating on him with somebody younger. The story was illustrated with a drawing of a dissipated-looking guy in a housecoat forlornly crushing a ginkgo leaf.

There was some thought by the editorial staff, which consisted largely of me, that we shouldn't print the story as being too scandalous. However, I thought as I crawled out from under the desk and shook the dust off my skirt, it was 1972 and if I aspired to make my mark in a modern field like broadcasting, a little controversy was all to the good. After all, I was a former crusading newspaper editor, so I shouldn't waste the opportunity to be a crusading literary magazine editor. When I got back to my dorm room, I defiantly placed "The Ginkgo Tree" and its illustration in the Accepted pile, thinking that this should fix everybody's little red wagon.

Then I grimly went to practice driving.

I had a learner's permit which meant somebody was supposed to be in the car with me. I decided not to bother with this. Instead, I went out to the parking lot behind New Dorm where I was unlikely to encounter heavy traffic and practiced circling.

Circling made me vaguely dizzy, and the experience was rendered a little surreal by the fact that Christmas music had started up on the radio. As I practiced pulling into a parking space, Karen Carpenter was singing "Merry Christmas, Darling," which included the immortal phrase, "Logs on the fire/ Fill me with desire."

"Sheesh," I said, turning off the radio.

I had a goal of getting my license before Christmas so Mama would not have to drive up and get me and so I could finish my Christmas shopping without having to be chauffeured around to the Mall. The problem was that I had developed a phobia about taking the driving test after I flunked it in Montgomery.

Finally, I had a great idea. I would go for my driving test in an out-of-the-way spot where the local cops weren't all that particular. I picked the nearby burg of Siluria, population roughly 200, and I had both Norman and Wayne ride with me. Barry had offered to come but he couldn't leave Clyde and I wasn't having a python in the car.

The trip to Siluria was uneventful except for me pulling out of a side road in front of an oncoming car which nonchalantly went around me without even beeping. Of my car's occupants, only Wayne freaked out. He tried to yell "Put on the brakes," but all that would come out was "Put!" Norman, who was reading a comic book, ignored the whole incident.

Eventually we arrived at the Siluria police station which was conveniently located under the water tank. The cop on duty was mildly surprised to see somebody turn up for the driving test, but he gamely climbed in the car, first ejecting Norman and Wayne, who were probably just as glad. I drove around downtown Siluria, stopping at the stop sign and signaling for all turns. Then it was time for the parallel parking test, which I had flunked in Montgomery by ramming the parallel parking car.

It's possible the cop was imbued with the spirit of Christmas, because after stating that I reminded him of his girlfriend, he said I didn't have to do parallel parking. I thanked him politely, collected Norman and Wayne and bought them both a Slushy at the Siluria Save-a-Stop.

It was a relief to be able to drive and I felt I could now devote the time I had spent practicing to figuring out my next career move.

Just before Christmas break I ran across something that could boost my television career and social life. I had been in the television studio going over the script for the student news report and cautioning Johnny Holman, our reporter for the day, that if he was going to refer to Arabs he shouldn't pronounce the word as AAY-Rabs. On the way out I glanced at the bulletin board. There in the column headed Summer Opportunities was a brochure for the Communications department at University of North Carolina, Chapel Hill.

Mr. Morrison, the studio director, was enthusiastic when I showed it to him. "They've got a state-of-the-art facility," he said happily. "It'd be quite a change for you," he gestured to take in the tiny studio which had one elderly camera. I kept the brochure.

On the drive to Montgomery, during which I heard "Merry Christmas, Darling" four times, I mulled. I was sure I could get admitted to Chapel Hill for the summer and if things worked out, I could transfer and graduate from there. It would practically ensure me a glamorous career in broadcasting.

Meanwhile, I could drive. If anybody wanted to look at Christmas lights, I'd be at the wheel.

When I pulled up in front of the house, Mama was standing on the porch. I rolled down the window.

"Where to?"

College Night

So far, 1973 was off to a great start. I had an apartment, and it was thanks to Mrs. Abernathy. I had been complaining pretty vociferously all along about wanting to move off campus, and finally Mrs. Abernathy proposed that I rent her Montevallo apartment, right across the street from campus. "I was keeping it for Susan Whitworth," she said, "but she's probably going to stay in England. She'll be graduating from high school early and it makes sense that she won't want to come back here for college."

I agreed that Susan Whitworth wouldn't want to come back here for college or anything else, and happily moved my stuff into the apartment. It was furnished in a style which reminded me of Jules Verne and included a great number of Mrs. Abernathy's tomb rubbings, lending the place a cultured yet gloomy air.

I now had a vaguely Egyptian-looking couch so people could come for a visit. Mama was my first guest. I had arranged for her to present a program on "Writing Your Book" for the English department and Mr. Morrison had suggested it be broadcast on campus television. Mama had seemed a little flustered during the presentation but she turned out to be preoccupied with something besides the book.

"Ray and Clay," she sighed. I nodded. Ray, as predicted, had flunked out of University of South Alabama and was back at home attending Auburn University's Montgomery branch. Clay had gotten his Ford fixed so that it drove forward, but that was the only good news on that front. To top things off, Mike Moran, known drug czar, had been arrested along with everybody who had been visiting his pad when the cops arrived. I said it was a good thing that Ray and Clay hadn't been there but Mama shook her head. "Jimmy says the police have started making deals with everybody they arrest for drugs. They want them to tell on all their friends." I pointed out that under the circumstances surely the jailbirds would tell on people they didn't like so all Ray and Clay had to do was stay on good terms with everybody. Despite my reassurances I could tell Mama wasn't optimistic.

To cheer her up, I took her over to see Dr. Atwater, the Dean of Men, who wanted a copy of *Dappled Sunshine*. He was very complimentary and confided in Mama that his own massive history of the Battle of First Manassas was expected to see publication before the end of the decade. I had noticed that Mama and Dr. Atwater had had their heads rather close together as she autographed the book to him, but after we got back to the car I was a little surprised to hear Mama say giddily, "Oh, he is so cute!" A chill went through me. The years had done little to diminish Mama's oomph. If she and Dr. Atwater ran off together, I would inevitably and unjustly be blamed, especially by Mrs. Atwater.

After Mama left I brooded over the situation, but didn't see what I could do. Besides, I had enough to worry about. I had been accepted to Chapel Hill for the summer but wasn't sure I actually wanted to go. I would, I decided, leave it up to Fate, or College Night.

College Night was a Montevallo tradition which made a whole lot more sense than Senior March, in which I was not planning to participate. For College Night the campus divided up into two teams and each side produced a musical. A panel of judges was imported from Birmingham, a place known for its theatrical sophistication. The winning side got bragging rights. The two teams were the Purple Cows and the Gold Lions. I was a backer of the Purples, on the grounds that Gold Lions was a lame name.

This year, I was the Purples' scriptwriter and was close to finishing what I believed to be the funniest script ever written on a college campus. A futuristic fantasy set on a spaceship, it involved a lot of cross-dressing jokes. I was aware that the subject might be controversial especially in light of "The Ginkgo Tree," but luckily the *Tower* wouldn't come out until after College Night was over. If, I told myself, the Purples won I would consider staying around Montevallo this summer, living in the Susan Whitworth memorial apartment and working in the English department. If through some miscarriage of justice the Purples lost, I was out of there.

Meanwhile, I was enjoying my new home. I now had a living room. When people came over, they didn't have to sit on the bed. Best of all, I had a kitchen. I cooked gourmet meals out of the *Betty Crocker Cookbook* I had gotten for high school graduation; dinner guests commented that I had a real feeling for chili. I was even able to save money on groceries by taking a plastic bag into the cafeteria and filling it up with salad and anything else that wouldn't spoil before I could get it into my refrigerator.

Having an apartment also simplified my work life. I could host meetings of the editorial staff of the *Tower* without having a dorm counselor burst in and arrest everybody for violating Closed Study Hours. And of course I could concentrate on polishing my College Night script, laughing heartily to myself as I typed another good one.

Then rehearsals started. There were two problems. The Purple leaders, Marcia and Warren Donlavy, were famous for being married and for having post-college ambitions involving the Birmingham Little Theatre. They expressed doubt about some of my funniest stuff. "I just don't know about the cross-dressing jokes," sighed Marcia. "I mean, you know Donald Beane is one of the judges and he's very sensitive." Donald Beane, who had been director of the Birmingham Little Theatre since before Pearl Harbor, was well known for his sensitivity, which had only increased in the wake of a recent item in the Birmingham paper linking his name with something unspecified that had happened in a public restroom.

"Phooey," I said. As a crusading literary magazine editor, I wasn't going to be scared of any Donald Beane.

In addition to Donald's sensitivity, the production was challenged by the fact that Dave Hollis, the male lead, had a tendency to show up drunk, once falling into the orchestra pit. Although Warren lectured him on professional responsibility, Dave managed to screw up dress rehearsal by tripping over the electrical cord to the set's hundreds of twinkling Christmas tree lights which were intended to represent the internal workings of a spaceship.

Finally came opening night. I was wearing Lyn's bridesmaid dress, of which I was starting to tire since I had had to wear it three weeks earlier for Honors Convocation. Nevertheless, as I plunked myself down in the front row, I was feeling confident.

Neither Dave nor anyone else seemed particularly drunk, and when the curtain went up the lights twinkled on cue, prompting applause from audience members who had never seen a Christmas light. My play, entitled *Ad Lib!* involved a society in which men were barred from careers in the space service under the theory that their lack of intuition rendered them unstable. The costume department had outdone itself in coming up with flashy spaceship uniforms, there were plenty of robots who could be counted on to clank onstage if things got dull, and the cast, despite being mostly sober, exhibited tremendous verve. The audience laughed heartily, especially at all the jokes about see-through pants. The curtain fell to tremendous applause and I smiled broadly.

Then came the Golds.

Their production, I was happy to note, wasn't much. It ran heavily to sorority girls wearing costumes which looked remarkably like fringed tablecloths. There was a good bit of tap dancing. Roughly every fifteen minutes, the heroine, known as Superbroad, would show up, announced by an ungodly outburst from the auditorium's huge, elderly Wurlitzer: "BLAAAAT!"

It was the custom of the judges to announce their verdict through some cute allusion to the winning side or play. Last year, since the Purple side had adopted the slogan "Purple Rain," in homage to the late Jimi Hendrix, the judges had simpered "It's Raining!"

Now they announced their decision:

"BLAAAAAT!"

That's it, I thought grimly. It's all over but the party.

Some time later, I tentatively opened one eye. The room was going around and around. Distressingly, it was also going over and over, like a Ferris wheel. I spotted a familiar tomb rubbing.

That narrowed things down; I was either in Susan Whitworth's former apartment or in a museum. I sat up. Yep, I was in the living room and the door was, happily, locked. I was rather unclear about how I had gotten there.

The Purple victory party, held in a hippie house close to campus, had not been very gleeful. Most of the attendees had concentrated on drowning their sorrows or otherwise altering their consciousness. Had brownies been involved? I was uncertain. The last thing I remembered was somebody handing me a Long Island Iced Tea which I drank right down since I was thirsty.

What, exactly, was in a Long Island Iced Tea?

I started to shake my head, giving up about halfway through the first shake.

At least one thing was certain. It was official; I was out of there.

Spring Break

To take my mind off the College Night fiasco, I invited the English Honors Society over for hot dogs. In the course of the festivities I started talking with Nancy Ann Crump, a big gawky girl who was running for editor of the *Alabamian*.

I offered her several pieces of good advice, the most important of which was to refrain from printing insulting jokes, even extremely funny ones, about the Dean of Women. As she was leaving, Nancy Ann said that she and a group of girls had rented a house in Panama City Beach for Spring Break and that I was welcome to come along.

Spring Break sounded like a real deal. According to Nancy Ann, the trip would cost $5 per day including food. A quick calculation confirmed that I couldn't even stay home for that. The bargain rate, said Nancy Ann, was due to two facts: the house she was renting was not exactly on the beach; and most of our food supply would involve a large ham which Nancy Ann was bringing.

That was okay with me. I liked ham.

Besides, I was sort of relieved I wouldn't be going to Montgomery. The only good news from home was that I hadn't had any bulletins about Mama running off with Dr. Atwater, so at least I had what the news was always calling "deniability." Otherwise, things continued to slide.

Over Christmas it had become obvious that the Montgomery situation had changed for the worse. Ray, joined by Clay if he happened to be on the outs with Louise, continued to annoy me by playing loud music. To make matters worse, Ray had acquired a taste for Existentialism. He went around quoting Nietzsche, whose name he mangled so badly that anyone hearing him automatically said "Gesundheit."

The atmosphere at home wasn't the only thing that had deteriorated. My friends from high school had drifted away or, in the case of the guys, been added to the Rejected Suitors list.

Annette, my childhood best friend, seemed to be spending an awful lot of time with her unhappily married boss, Ricky. Our telephone conversations had degenerated into a monologue on the unfairness of the Vatican's policy on divorce. As for Patty Harris, she claimed to be cutting a wide swath through the sorority scene at Alabama and had traded her Volkswagen Beetle for an Audi. At least she had shut up about the jade engagement ring.

I was packing to leave for the beach when I had a phone call from Mrs. Abernathy. She had a problem. I wondered if she had lost her house key, but the dilemma turned out to involve a conference of foreign student leaders set for next week in Birmingham. She had forgotten that Susan Whitworth was supposed to handle registration. Susan Whitworth seemed to have forgotten, too, since she was currently in London. Could I help?

It would mean cutting my Spring Break short, but I didn't see that I had much choice. I wanted to make sure I kept my student job just in case things in Chapel Hill didn't work out and I had to return to Montevallo in the fall.

Muttering, I finished packing and set out for Panama City Beach.

The house Nancy Ann had rented turned out to be five blocks from the beach. It was old and beat-up but it had plenty of room and a full kitchen. Somebody had brought a radio and "Crocodile Rock" was blasting as I bopped around unpacking. Besides Nancy Ann and me, our group included a sociology major named Susie Faulk whose wardrobe leaned toward the hippie; Ann Donnelly, an art major; and two sisters named Jo and Joyce Hammond, both business majors.

I thought idly that we should have included a home ec major, ideally one specializing in ham. We had just finished unpacking and were hauling out our swimsuits when the crisis hit.

There was no ham.

Nancy Ann dumped everything out of the grocery bag, then turned it upside down and shook it. Still no ham. "I don't understand," she cried in anguish. "Mama said she'd pack it."

Then, noting some impending hostility, Nancy Ann rallied and announced Plan B.

"Tina Antonio said to call her on the first rainy day and she'd have us over for dinner."

Tina Antonio was from Panama City and was spending Spring Break with her mother who, said Nancy Ann, made a mean lasagna. It was agreed that it might rain tomorrow, so we calmed down and trekked to the beach, after which we ate the bacon and eggs which had been intended for tomorrow's breakfast.

The next morning it was indeed raining, and after making toast with all the leftover bread, we waited with bated breath as Nancy Ann called Tina.

"Well, here it is," said Nancy Ann into the phone. "Raining. Yep, looks like it will rain all day."

She listened for a couple of seconds, then hung up, looking bewildered. "All she said was, 'sure is.'"

It later developed that Tina had forgotten to alert her mother, who was every bit as mean as her lasagna and not at all keen on surprises, and had been too chicken to admit it to Nancy Ann.

Nevertheless, there we were.

After a brief, acrimonious discussion it was agreed that we would pool whatever money we had and go get enough food to last us through the day, after which we would think of something.

We made a brief, soggy trip to the grocery store for peanut butter and another loaf of bread. After lunch the rain quit and we slogged back to the beach and sat under the pier where the sand wasn't so wet. It looked like I wasn't going to be missing much by leaving early.

On the walk back, Susie came up with a good idea. "Look, man!" she said excitedly, pointing to a notice on a phone pole. On the following day, there was going to be a fish fry in Mexico Beach, a little town about ten miles away. Jo and Joyce, who were in charge of the funds, announced that we had enough money for fish, which would be a welcome change from peanut butter. Besides, maybe there would be a whole lot of fish and we could take leftovers home.

The next day was sunny and after we finished our toast we headed for Mexico Beach. There was a huge long line for fish and we were pretty much starved by the time we got our plates, which we attacked with the vigor usually associated with grizzlies coming out of hibernation.

There weren't going to be any leftovers.

Just then, Ann yelled "Gary!" There, eating a large chunk of mullet, was Gary White, treasurer of Montevallo's chapter of Lambda Chi fraternity. Gary finished swallowing and greeted Ann joyfully. He and eleven of his fraternity brothers were staying in a house in Mexico

Beach, he said, but the stove didn't work so they were lunching out.

At this point, a squadron of frat boys arrived with bad news. They had been evicted. It developed that their landlady, apparently a fiend from hell, had taken exception to being criticized for having a nonworking stove and had thrown them out on a trumped-up charge of "sitting on the bed."

I felt there might be more to the story, but the bottom line was that we needed food and they needed shelter. In the background, somebody's radio began playing "I Can See Clearly Now."

There was a brief meeting and following practically no discussion a plan took shape.

I was appointed doorkeeper. As the first carload of frat boys pulled into the driveway, I adopted a businesslike demeanor.

Halt," I said. They halted. "There's a cover charge," I elaborated. "You can't come in here unless you give us some money or something to eat or drink."

The frat boys went into a huddle and came out with an offer of five beers and fourteen dollars, which I readily accepted since they had taken the precaution of handing me one of the beers.

Following a conference between Jo and Joyce and the frat business majors, it was decided that the Nancy Ann contingent would retain rights to the bedrooms and that people who wound up having to sleep on the porch would receive a refund.

I had never been around many frat boys since at Montevallo there weren't enough guys to go around in the first place. When you added in the fact that I didn't belong to a sorority, I was as likely to meet a frat boy as an alligator. I wasn't sure if this bunch was typical but if so the Lambdas were a jolly lot. They had bounced back from their eviction determined to party even heartier.

Some of them were also practical. A guy named Steve, one of their business majors, suggested we make a batch of Purple Jesus. This economical punch was very popular in some circles, though Steve admitted the proportions would need to be tweaked. Since Purple Jesus was usually mixed up in a 55-gallon drum, the original recipe called for five gallons of Pure Grain Alcohol and fifty gallons of Welch-Ade. After some input from Frank, a math major, it was agreed that one gallon of Pure Grain Alcohol and five gallons of Welch-Ade would work, and a delegation was sent to Ace Hardware for a plastic kitchen garbage can.

Thanks to the fraternity's groceries, we now had plenty to eat and drink and since Purple Jesus contained grape juice a cupful probably counted as a serving of fruit. The only real casualty of the day's events was Susie, who overindulged before setting out to walk to Miracle Strip Amusement Park, some miles away. When we finally found her, she was suffering from a colossal sunburn and had to be packed in ice.

The next day continued sunny and we divided our time among the beach, the Miracle Strip, and the Purple Jesus. Susie sat under the pier; Frank sprayed her with Solarcaine.

Spring Break had been an interesting experience, I thought, and it would not surprise me if romance blossomed between some members of our impromptu house party.

I would not, of course, be there to see it. I had to go to work.

As I drove away, some of the guys were putting up a volleyball net and "Love Train" was playing on the radio.

I had plenty of time to think on the way back. This summer, I decided, I would not even look for a part-time job. I would arrive at Chapel Hill ready to concentrate on my television career and, incidentally, to enjoy just being a college student.

When I got back to Montevallo and took stock, I found some consolation: Spring Break had netted me a profit of four dollars and half a watermelon.

Overcommitted

At least I wasn't the editor of the *Alabamian* anymore. My job as editor of the *Tower* paid less, but was a whole lot less trouble, especially since the *Tower* only came out once per year, rather than every time I turned around. My only concern was whether "The Ginkgo Tree" would be considered too radical for Montevallo.

Meanwhile, I was still being run ragged, but now it was by more interesting stuff.

Besides, I was still enjoying having an apartment. My home was handy for hosting editorial meetings of the *Tower*, planning the activities of the Science Fiction Club, stacking up the papers and books I had to research as part of my job with the English department, organizing my notes for the freelance articles I wrote for the Montgomery newspaper, planning my summer at Chapel Hill, completing all the extra work required by the course overload I was taking, and last but not least for providing a kitchen table and floor on which I could place the piles of stuff required by my volunteer work with the *Star Trek* Welcommittee.

By this time, *Star Trek* had officially been off the air for four years, but because it had immediately gone into syndicated reruns and was currently on every afternoon at 3:30 (another obligation I had worked into my schedule) there was an apparently never-ending stream of teenagers writing to NBC about their loyalty to the show. There the matter would have rested if not for *Star Trek* fandom. At some point somebody had decided that all these nerds who wrote NBC had to be put in touch with the many exciting activities to which liking *Star Trek* entitled them, such as the opportunity to pay to attend science fiction conventions. I couldn't remember why I had originally volunteered to be part of the Welcommittee, but the end result was that every two weeks I received a big manila envelope of letters I had to answer, commiserating with the writers about the fact that *Star Trek* was no longer filming new episodes and pointing them in the direction of the Leonard Nimoy Fan Club or whatever.

One beautiful afternoon in April, I was lugging my envelope of unanswered *Star Trek* letters around with me, planning to answer them if I could find a free moment. This wasn't going to be easy. First, I had Spanish class, where we were slowly reading a book whose title roughly translated to *A Cold Night in Lima* and which most of the students called *A Cold Day in Hell* since it was boring. As soon as the bell rang I had to run across campus to my job in the English department.

When I skidded through the door, Angela Warner, the other student worker, was attempting to answer the phone. "Eng Eng Eng," she stated. The phone was on speaker; the person on the other end of the line had already moved on to "Hi Angela, is Mrs. Abernathy in?" "Eng Eng Eng," continued Angela, nothing daunted. The person on the other end got bored and hung up. "Huh," said Angela indignantly. "Th th th they hu hu hung."

"Yeah," I said. "Have you seen Mrs. Abernathy?" Angela had enough sense to shake her head.

Mrs. Abernathy had apparently forgotten to show up for office hours again. On the one hand, this wasn't good because in addition to teaching she was producing, writing, and narrating the campus educational television series *Great Art and Literature* for which I had to find and organize all the visuals, and this week's episode was already going to be late. On the other hand, it was great since as soon as I got all the pictures of St. George and the Dragon or whatever arranged on her desk and floor, I could yank out those *Star Trek* letters and get them answered on the English department typewriter.

If Mrs. Abernathy had shown up, I would have been kept busy finding her car keys, retrieving her class roll from the refrigerator or wherever she had left it, helping her grade the freshman term papers, and—this had happened last week— writing a script about Beowulf. "You're a lifesaver!" she would say as I handed her the reading glasses, grade book or rabies certificate she had lost. "I don't know what this department would do without you!"

I wished the *Star Trek* Welcommittee was as appreciative. Although I had gotten a note from Star Fleet Command, which was the organization officially in charge of the Welcommittee, saying "We rely on our true fans like you to spread the word," the word they wanted me to spread was that the next science fiction convention would be held in Philadelphia and that tickets were $35 or $45 at the door. Besides that, I was getting really annoyed with my *Star Trek* Welcommittee crew captain.

This was the little jerk responsible for sending me the manila envelope full of letters every two weeks. His name was Timmy and he seemed to have confused himself with the actual Captain Kirk. In his last cover letter, he had outdone himself, ordering me regally to answer these fan letters "and pretty damn quickly, if you please." Brave words, I fumed, from somebody who probably gets his butt kicked every time he dresses out for gym. I typed angrily away until I finished replying to all the fan letters, at which time I realized that since Mrs. Abernathy hadn't appeared I was going to get to leave work on time.

As I headed out the door, Dr. Tyler, who taught History of English Literature, was regaling Angela with his original poem about Watergate, written in the style of *The Canterbury Tales*. I was really getting bored with this Nixon stuff, though Angela seemed to appreciate Dr. Tyler's effort.

I ambled over to the Student Union Building, checked my post office box, dumped my stack of *Star Trek* Welcommittee letters into the outgoing mail and fought my way out through the gaggle of hippies who had lately begun infesting the front steps.

My mail included a postcard from Susan Whitworth saying "London is great!" and noting that some big shot with the BBC had taken an interest in her. I also had a letter from Mama, which I read as I walked. *Dappled Sunshine* continued to sell well and Mama had been interviewed on the local Public Radio station. Otherwise, the news wasn't cheerful. Ray had already managed to get on academic probation. Clay was having unspecified trouble at his job. Dingbat had bitten the vet.

Brooding, I flopped down onto a bench. I would need to give Mama a reassuring phone call tonight, though I had no idea what I was going to say. It occurred to me that I was getting myself in much the same situation as Mama, who was still spending her free time caretaking her gang of helpless old ladies, only I wasn't limiting myself to old ladies. I was beginning to suspect that I had too many people relying on me. The whole Science Fiction Club, the English department, the *Tower*, and, even if they wouldn't admit it, the *Star Trek* Welcommittee. My eyes narrowed. I was, I decided, going to demand a leave of absence from the Welcommittee for the summer. I wasn't even planning to have a student job while at Chapel Hill, and I sure wasn't going to be fooling with any Welcommittee while I was supposed to be concentrating on my career. If Cap'n Timmy didn't like it, I thought happily, I had the perfect rejoinder: "Dear Cap'n Timmy, blow it out Uranus."

That would fix him.

I sat for a moment dreamily contemplating a summer in which I wouldn't be driven crazy by everybody's conflicting demands. Then, a feeling of unease gradually crept over me. Wasn't there somewhere I should be right now? I thought. Well, not in class. Spanish was the last thing I had today. The Science Fiction Club didn't meet again until Thursday. Since Mrs. Abernathy had forgotten to show up I wasn't working late in the English department. I'd already finished going through the galley proofs of the *Tower*. I looked at my watch. It was 3:12. It took me five minutes to walk to my apartment. *Star Trek* didn't come on till 3:30. I had thirteen free minutes and no idea what to do with them.

I spent a few more minutes tranquilly envisioning a relaxing summer, before suddenly realizing I was sitting under the crabapple tree, which was in full bloom. This tree was considered the most romantic spot on campus (the most romantic public spot, anyway) and had been the scene of as many as a dozen proposals over the last fifty years. The bench was a favorite spot for courting couples. In fact, out of the corner of my eye I spotted a courting couple glaring furtively at me, mentally urging me to move along since I obviously had no business there. Elaborately ignoring them, I looked at my watch again.

I wasn't going anywhere. I still had three minutes.

Watergate Does Not Bother Me

I rolled up at Chapel Hill on June 1, 1973, and the first thing I noticed was the hippies. There were flocks of them, wandering around amiably or lying on the grass.

Luckily, McIver Dorm didn't seem overpopulated with hippies, although the residents of my hall were something of a mixed bag. We had students from Taiwan who were working on the new Chinese dictionary, a black girl named Vina Bowes who was reported to be a dangerous radical, and Amy Towles, a committed feminist who reminded me a little of Lana except for the hair. She roomed with Brenda Mizer, who looked a lot like Natalie Wood and who had, according to Amy, a mean boyfriend.

I was taking three courses: Shakespeare, History of Cinema, and scriptwriting. Shakespeare was pretty entertaining. The teacher, Ms. Hollis, was the next best thing to a hippie. She gave lectures while prowling around, occasionally shaking her fringe to make a point. There was at least one official hippie in the class, a guy named Martin who expressed his sympathy for King Lear: "He was going through some changes, man, His plans went all ascrew." History of Cinema, taught by Dr. Arthur, an old guy who looked like he used to date Clara Bow, was interesting too, since we spent all class period watching movies.

Then there was scriptwriting.

It should have been great. The problem was the teacher. Mr. Hashim was a beady-eyed, hyper type who jumped around a lot but without Ms. Hollis' sense of style. He was sort of an evil version of Marvin Plotnick and appeared to consider correctly that we were a captive audience for his impersonations of Milton Berle. He didn't like anything anybody wrote. When he had us adapt a story about alcoholic shoplifters for the screen, he said my script was too romantic and gave Rachel Saperstein, who sat behind me, a C for too many commas. "God damn Muslim," hissed Rachel, who kept up with international politics. I wasn't sure about Mr. Hashim being a Muslim but had no trouble believing the more disquieting rumor that he had been a patient in the state hospital for the criminally insane. He probably escaped, I thought gloomily. I wondered if the hospital had a telephone hotline.

Once I got out of Hashim's class, I faced another menace. I had to walk through the Arb. The Chapel Hill Arboretum had once been a tranquil place in which to commune with nature between classes. Then, some years earlier, a female student had been murdered there. The Arb was the natural shortcut to all class buildings, but nobody, including me, liked going in there even in broad daylight. I always ran.

I knew that when I reached McIver Dorm, I would face disappointment.

I was used to watching *Star Trek* reruns every afternoon. After I finished my first day of classes, I had happily cranked up the television to find John Chancellor intoning "What did he know, and when did he know it?"

Watergate. On all channels.

From what I had been able to gather, Watergate started when Nixon told some Cubans to burglarize the Democrats. The Cubans had unfortunately gotten caught. Then Nixon bribed the FBI to spy on the CIA and after that he took part in the coverup. To top things off, it now appeared that he had tape recorded himself hatching his nefarious schemes.

"Sheesh," I said. Really, if I wasn't any better than that at being crooked, I would never have run for President. Meanwhile, John Chancellor was just getting warmed up. It was time for Jeb Stuart Magruder, whose appearance was always announced with a degree of vim usually reserved for Johnny Carson:

"Jeb...Stuart...Magruder!!!!!!"

"Sheesh," I reiterated, turning off the set.

In the hall, I bumped into Amy. "Come on," she said. "We've got to avenge Brenda."

"Huh?" I said. It turned out Amy had convened a meeting of everybody on the hall except the Chinese students and Brenda to decide the proper response to the latest atrocity committed by Brenda's boyfriend Billy. His evil deed of the week had involved canceling a date with Brenda, who thought they were going to dinner for her birthday, in order to wax his car. Brenda was crying her eyes out, said Amy censoriously, when she should have been plotting revenge.

After a little discussion, it was decided we should go egg his car as soon as it got dark. Unfortunately, I was appointed to drive the getaway car. Vina declined to participate on the grounds that since she was black we would blame the whole enterprise on her. This was actually a good idea and I was rather sorry she had thought of it first.

"We need the Chinese students," I said, carefully explaining that I was only interested in their groceries, not in blaming the whole thing on them. The Chinese students cooked some really odd things and they were heavily into fish.

The Chinese student who had told me to call her Rose answered the door. "Hi Rose," I said brightly. "Do you happen to have any rotten fish?" After correcting Rose's initial impression that I had been reduced to begging for food, I added, "We're going to go throw garbage on this guy's car because he's been asking for it. Uh—" I continued, in an effort to be polite, "do you want to come?"

It turned out she did. This presented something of a quandary, since if Rose got arrested it would probably put a huge crimp in the Chinese dictionary project. I would, I decided, have to stick to Rose like glue.

Amy knew where Billy lived and furthermore had seen his car. There it was, looking freshly waxed. Our supplies included, in addition to the rotten fish, some actual rotten eggs and a half quart of sour milk contributed by Vina. I had suggested that I stay behind the wheel since I was the getaway driver, but had been howled down on the grounds that I would drive off and leave them.

"Whatever," I said, hauling my bag of stuff and Rose out of the car.

"Okay, Rose," I hissed. "Stick close to me and if I say 'run,' you run." Rose nodded.

The mission was an unqualified success except the part where I fell over the rosebush. Amy was very happy with the outcome, saying that striking back against our oppressors would empower all of us. Actually, Rose was the only one who seemed empowered; her adventure made her the toast of the local Taiwanese community.

At any rate, there were no repercussions. Either Billy never told Brenda about it or Brenda thought it was better not to say anything.

Speaking of repercussions, I had been monitoring my mail pretty closely since I expected to receive feedback after the *Tower* printed the controversial story "The Ginkgo Tree." I had heard absolutely nothing by the time I left Montevallo and now decided that either nobody had read the story or that readers had thought it was really about a tree.

A couple of days after the egging mission, I got good news in the mail, though not from home. According to Mama's worried letters, the only positive news from Montgomery was that Dingbat hadn't bitten anybody lately. My other correspondents were more cheerful. Annette wrote with happy tidings that Ricky had secured a divorce from his mean wife and was amenable to the idea of trying for an annulment. Wayne was writing me weekly with news from the world of science fiction. I wondered if it would be premature to add him to my list of Rejected Suitors. Annie Gruen Fields wanted me to come visit at the Gulf.

Susan Whitworth kept up a stream of postcards from London where she was interning with the BBC. The first couple were cheerful. Then the tune changed. "London hectic," said the most recent one which featured a photo of Waterloo Bridge. Then I opened a letter from Cousin Kate. She was inviting me for a visit. Kate Ferguson McPherson was a distant cousin of my mother's. We had discovered her living in Cameron, the little North Carolina town from which Mama's ancestors had moved, God knows why, to Mississippi.

I loved visiting Cousin Kate. Her house, in which she lived by herself, was a huge Victorian pile complete with lots of porches, balconies, and turrets. It had been her childhood home. She had moved around with her husband, who was a mine supervisor, but on his death had come back to Cameron to live.

Though she was in her eighties, Cousin Kate was temperamentally the opposite of the helpless old bats Mama usually wound up babysitting. Not only was she independent, she was interesting. She had trained as a botanist and was almost as entertaining as Euell Gibbons when it came to eating weird things.

On the day of my visit, for lunch we had boiled violets, a daylily casserole, and haggis. The haggis, she explained, had been a door prize. I glanced uneasily at the haggis, which was gray. I decided to eat it since if I succeeded I would never have to worry about famine. I managed by swallowing it without chewing.

Cousin Kate and I spent a happy afternoon touring the house and grounds. Then, after it got dark, she surprised me by saying "Go upstairs, go in all the rooms, then come back down and tell me which one is haunted."

"Urk," I said, but proceeded upstairs where I stared into each room in a gingerly fashion.

When I hurriedly returned downstairs, I said "That middle room on the left?" Cousin Kate nodded happily.

Really, it had been pretty unmistakable. Even though the house wasn't air conditioned and it was roughly 200 degrees up there, when I peered in the room I had felt cold. It turned out that Cousin Kate was merely confirming that I, like all Fergusons, had second sight. Luckily, whatever was haunting the upstairs never bothered coming down, and I spent a peaceful night followed by a hearty breakfast of cattail roots.

Back on campus, I felt empowered. Cousin Kate was an ideal role model. She wasn't afraid of anything in this world or the next. She probably wouldn't even be afraid of walking through the Arb.

I happily put my suitcase down on the bed and switched on the television.

"Jeb...Stuart...Magruder!!!!!!!!!"

As I switched off the set, I shook my head. Why couldn't his parents have just named him Mike?

Everybody Must Get Stoned

As the summer wore on, hippies were everywhere I looked; kind of like Woodstock without the rain. As for pot, things had reached the point that if I was walking across the Quad with Amy or somebody and happened to say "hi" to a guy, he would immediately pull out a joint and suggest we all have a smoke. I continued to tell people I had asthma and Amy habitually refused on grounds of feminism, but it was still kind of annoying having to cross campus in a cloud of smoke, as if we were going to school in a forest fire. The pot contingent was particularly numerous around the post office, probably because the steps were handy for lounging.

I was still getting a lot of mail. Wayne continued to write every week and we were now signing our letters "love," so I was unsure whether to leave him on the Rejected Suitors list. Lyn wrote with tales of La Jolla. She was apparently still thinking of herself as lucky since she sounded perky and said they would take me to Haight-Ashbury when I came out, so I could see some hippies. Cousin Kate sent a thank you note for the book *Cooking with Flowers*. The news from home was uniformly bad and since Mama and I wrote each other nearly every day, there was a lot of it. Clay was back with Louise but had lost his job; Ray had taken to staying out overnight and Mama didn't know if he was getting his insulin. Dingbat had bitten the postman.

On one of my trips to the post office, I received the weirdest missive yet from Susan Whitworth. It was a postcard of the Tower of London and on the back was written "I am not a whore."

Who's accusing you? I thought exasperatedly. I wondered if Susan Whitworth might have been stoned when she wrote it, though I had never heard of stoned people feeling compelled to send postcards. Everybody around here just acted like a jerk and ate Fritos.

My classes continued to be a mixed bag. I made an A on my Romeo and Juliet paper and in History of Cinema I was doggedly viewing my way through Ingmar Bergman, almost always remembering not to call him Ingrid Bergman.

Meanwhile, scriptwriting had gotten worse. Hashim had given up on Milton Berle and was now spending class time regaling us with whole chapters from his unpublished novel about religious serial killers, entitled *Honk if You Love Jesus*. Nobody laughed during his presentations, which should have given him a clue that he might as well forget about eventually selling the film rights. Rachel was still insisting that Hashim had it in for her because she was Jewish. I was still reassuring her that Hashim was equal opportunity and was being an asshole to everybody. Beyond Hashim, the problem with the class was that I couldn't stand any of my fellow students except Rachel and a guy named Lonnie who was convinced that Hashim had it in for him because he was gay.

I couldn't think why Hashim didn't get along with the rest of the students since they were easily as obnoxious as he was. Two of the worst were the married couple who always dressed alike. Since it was summer, they were partial to white linen with matching sunglasses. If I had been there in winter, I assumed they would have shown up in identical raccoon coats, probably accessorized with earmuffs. They didn't like Hashim, which was good, but other than that you couldn't talk to them about anything but Francis Ford Coppola. That was the problem, really. Everybody in the class but me seemed headed for Hollywood, except for a couple who said Hollywood was dead and the real action was in Portugal.

Meanwhile, I was supposed to be talking to the Admissions office about transferring, but somehow I never got around to it. Once I was all set to go when a bunch of people suddenly asked if I wanted to see *Paper Moon*. Once Vina came back from her SNCC meeting with a whole plate of leftover chocolate chip cookies.

Once Watergate sort of intervened. Jeb Stuart Magruder was still making my viewing hours a living hell, but one afternoon as I was headed out the door I impulsively switched on the television to find that Watergate had taken the day off in favor of a *Star Trek* episode that I had only seen six or seven times. I'd get around to the Admissions office eventually, I decided.

Things around the dorm had calmed down. Brenda had perked up some since we egged Billy's car but that might have been a coincidence. One Saturday, she was supposed to go to the Mall with me but the day dawned so bright and sunny that Brenda felt our time could more profitably be spent at the pool. It was okay with me since the pool was within walking distance. Because Brenda had stopped talking about Billy, we mostly sat in silence while I read my *Cosmo*. Thanks to scientific advances in the world of sunscreen, I was now able to stay out in the sun as much as thirty minutes without burning, so I was enjoying myself. I had just finished an article entitled "Should You Marry Down?" when I became aware of a group of people sitting near us. They were all reading and a couple were making notes, ignoring the occasional splash of water from the pool's friskier occupants. They were maybe the quietest bunch I had seen at Chapel Hill, so I poked Brenda. "Who're they?" Brenda shrugged, "Law students."

None of them were wearing matching outfits, which was a major point in their favor.

It was shortly after this weekend that the crisis occurred. McIver Dorm didn't have air conditioning, which was a mistake, but we all had phones in our rooms. Mine never rang, until one evening in early August.

It was Mama. Ray and Clay had been arrested. Mama had come home one evening to find Louise and Dingbat hiding in the garage, having escaped the raid by the skin of their teeth. The cops had had a warrant and had apparently known what they were looking for; Louise said sadly that Mike Moran must have ratted them out. Jimmy had helped Mama get Ray and Clay out of jail, but she had had to mortgage the house to make bail. This was a severe blow. My father had paid cash for the house, back in the late 1940s. Unless Mama succeeded in riding herd on Ray and Clay until their court date, she could lose the family home.

I said something soothing and hung up, but I now faced a dilemma. It was becoming obvious that I wasn't cut out for further television courses at Chapel Hill since I had no guarantee that the insane asylum would come take Hashim back anytime soon.

I could, I thought, go back to Montevallo. Luckily I hadn't said anything to Mrs. Abernathy about my original plan to transfer to Chapel Hill, so I had my apartment and job in the English department waiting for me. If I were at Montevallo I would be only ninety minutes from Montgomery in case Mama needed reinforcements, and the situation had plainly escalated to the point where she was probably going to need help.

Plus, Wayne and I had written faithfully all summer and we had a lot in common since we both liked *Star Trek*. Maybe I was fated to go back to Montevallo and marry Wayne.

It would be kind of a relief to have that settled, but what about going to law school?

No, I didn't want to, but after being around Chapel Hill's particular batch of television students, I was beginning to think twice about my career choice.

I needed a sign.

I was mulling the problem a couple of days later in the library's nonfiction section, a place I liked to go because it had the biggest globe of the world I had ever seen. I gave the globe a surreptitious spin, ignoring the Do Not Touch notice. Maybe the globe would stop on Montevallo.

It stopped on Madagascar.

I gave the ceiling a meaningful look, since I was afraid to say "quit fooling around" out loud.

"I need a sign," I said firmly.

My way out led through the botany section. I spotted a book sticking halfway out of a shelf and leaned over to examine the title. *Edible Plants of the Southeast.* This reminded me of Cousin Kate, so I pulled the book out and flipped it open.

Somebody had been careless. This book was supposed to be on Interlibrary Loan.

Inside the cover, in all caps, was the notice PLEASE RETURN TO UNIVERSITY OF MONTEVALLO.

I looked at the ceiling again.

"Okay," I said. "I'm going."

Student Defender

Everything was gone.

The apartment went first. I was at Mama's going through my fall clothes when the phone rang.

It was Susan Whitworth. "Hi!" I said, astonished that she was calling me from England.

"How's London?"

Susan Whitworth laughed. "Oh, I'm not in London," she said brightly.

She was in Montevallo. She was in her apartment. What did I want her to do with my stuff?

Though rendered speechless, I found I could still think. The stuff in question consisted of my winter coat, a couple of sweaters, my cookbook and a box of *Star Trek* Welcommittee records. I managed to say that I would pick the stuff up, or if she didn't mind bringing it to the English department I could just get it at work.

There was a brief, sinister silence.

Okay, I understood that even though I had paid rent, Susan Whitworth considered the apartment hers. The same could not be said, I felt, for the job. What was the English department thinking?

How could a person who was technically still in high school possibly manage a responsible position that on any given day included writing scripts, grading papers, and finding car keys?

Bitterly, I considered asking Susan Whitworth if by any chance she had gotten engaged to Wayne in the last few days, thus screwing me out of my matrimonial prospects, but I didn't want to give her any ideas. Instead, I stated briefly that I would come by the apartment to collect the pitiful remnants of a happier life, and hung up the phone with considerable vigor.

After spending a moment gathering my wits, I called the University housing office. They were used to hearing from me since I switched rooms so often, and I was able to talk myself into a private room in Hanson, an older dorm in a convenient location. It wasn't forever, I thought. I would be graduating at the end of the fall semester.

Nevertheless, I still had to have a job.

When I got back to Montevallo, I stuffed my fall clothes into the dorm room's closet and headed across campus to look for work. I needed an immediate paycheck, and that meant only one thing.

The cafeteria.

Since nobody in their right mind would work there, the cafeteria was always hiring. The manager, Ms. Neuffer, was either a German war bride or an escaped Nazi war criminal. She was happy enough to hire me, though, since I was willing to work behind the scenes.

This meant mopping, but it was better than having anybody see me slinging hash. After being shown where the bucket was, I took my leave and headed grimly to my former apartment.

Susan Whitworth opened the door. I was appalled.

Her hair had been chopped off. Susan Whitworth's long red hair had been one of the attributes, though not the main one, responsible for garnering her so much male attention.

"Oh, this?" she asked, indicating her head. "Trying a new look. Here you go," she added, shoving my box of stuff at me and shutting the door.

I never did figure out exactly what had happened to Susan Whitworth in London. Mrs. Abernathy, who was teaching my English honors seminar, said airily that over the summer it had just become obvious to Susan Whitworth that her real interests lay elsewhere than in television.

Meanwhile, I had other things to worry about.

My romance with Wayne never really got off the ground. We had a couple of dates, but at a certain point it became apparent that mutual admiration for Ray Bradbury was not a solid foundation for a relationship. Besides that, I was troubled by a vision of me at my wedding, stoically telling my bridesmaid that after all, things could be worse.

The news from home contained a bright spot. Ray and Clay had not attempted to escape, and Jimmy felt confident he could get them off on a technicality. Instead of me receiving gloomy news from home, it appeared that from now on, home would receive gloomy news from me.

Time passed. I was getting increasingly tired of mopping.

Law school loomed in the distance.

Watergate was still showing on all channels.

Things were bleak. Had the universe actually been trying to tell me to go to Madagascar?

In need of spiritual sustenance, I sought out the geode. As I sat meditatively in front of it, ignoring the geology students eating lunch, I reflected sadly that maybe Mama was right. Maybe we were put in this world to help others. That still didn't explain what the others were there for, unless they were just there to torment me. However, although it was obvious that my life was headed down the drain, if I helped others it wouldn't have been a total waste.

I would, I decided, go to law school and afterwards plan to become a legal missionary, probably in Madagascar.

I got up, brushing off my jeans. I would go right now and find somebody to help.

First I would get myself a milkshake.

As I ambled across the snack bar with my shake, I spotted somebody who needed my help. There at a table sat Nancy Ann Crump, recently elected editor of the *Alabamian*. An important part of Nancy Ann's platform was her pledge to liven up the newspaper's masthead, yet now she seemed unable to decide about typefaces. She was in fact frowning at a sheet of samples. "Hi!" I said helpfully, sitting down. "Here, let me help you with those." Nancy Ann looked a little confused but handed me the sheet and we were deep in a discussion of Times New Roman when a shadow fell over the table.

It was Bob England, last seen presenting a 21-gun salute to the streaking Marty Holbeck.

Whatever Bob was planning to say went unspoken, since Nancy Ann deflected him with "Kathie's going to law school, too."

"Really!" said Bob. "I'm taking the LSAT in Birmingham next month."

"Me too," I said, a little surprised.

"Are you working with the paper this semester?" asked Bob, trying to look at the sheet of typefaces.

"No, I'm just looking at a few fonts," I said, covering the sheet with my hand.

Bob's eyes narrowed. "So you don't have a student job this semester?"

"No," I lied since there was no way he could have seen me in the kitchen.

"Well, listen," said Bob. It developed that he had, God knows why, been appointed Student Defender and that he had a budget for an assistant at $150 per semester. "Interested?" he asked.

"Sure!" I said. I decided that I didn't have to give notice at the cafeteria. They would figure out I had quit when they never saw me again.

Bob stood up to leave, explaining importantly that he had to go plea bargain, but then he stopped. "Are you dating anybody?" Well, no. It turned out Bob wanted to fix me up on a blind date with a friend of his, a lawyer who lived in Atlanta. "Okay," I said.

After Bob left, Nancy Ann weighed in. "I'm sorry," she said, shaking her head. "I didn't mean to get you mixed up with Bob. He's so bossy. I was just waiting for him to criticize our typefaces. And I mean, you certainly don't want a date with—"

"Sure I do," I said.

The blind date with Bob's friend Jack was set for the evening of the day I would take the LSAT. I thought happily that after I finished the test I would go by the Mall and get myself something attractive to wear.

Meanwhile, I spent my time getting ready for the LSAT and working with Bob. Being an assistant student defender involved listening to a lot of flimsy excuses as to why the defendant in question had been caught planting kudzu in front of the campus police station, but it beat hell out of mopping.

Besides, as Bob pointed out, we never lost a case.

Then came the morning of the LSAT. When I arrived at Birmingham's Samford University, I discovered to my horror that all the buildings looked alike. After several nightmarish circuits of the campus I picked the most likely-looking building, parked the car in the fire lane, and ran inside. I had guessed right. The test itself paled in comparison.

However, after I finished the LSAT my nerves were shattered and I felt unequal to driving to the Mall. I would, I thought, go straight back to Montevallo and try to recover my equilibrium.

I got back to Hanson to discover that I had very little fit to wear. I had spent too much time on studying and too little on improving my wardrobe. Other than jeans, everything in the closet was torn, dirty, or missing except for Lyn's bridesmaid dress and a brown plaid pantsuit. "Okay," I said bitterly, jerking the pantsuit off the hanger. It was a shame, I thought, that one who had once been fashion forward should be reduced to this. To top things off, my eyelids were swollen. I would have to wear my glasses.

Jack Purser turned out to be a friendly guy who also wore glasses, though that didn't count since he was a guy. He had met Bob when Jack was a dorm counselor and Bob a student at Samford. I explained about all the buildings looking alike. Jack nodded, adding that as an underclassman Bob had gotten lost several times, even though he claimed to have an excellent sense of direction.

I felt we understood each other.

We went to see *American Graffiti* in Birmingham. At a certain point, I realized I was having a good time. I couldn't remember the last time that had happened though I thought it was probably when I egged Billy's car. As we arrived back on campus it suddenly dawned on me that it was after curfew and that the dorm would be locked. "Augh," I said. "I'm going to have to get Pam to let me in."

Getting back into Hanson after curfew involved beating on the window of Pam Steele, who was the nervous type and a Yankee to boot, but whose room was right next to the side door.

Tonight, after a prolonged volley of knocks, I still couldn't see Pam. Jack went to look through the side door's window. There was a muffled outcry from within. Pam, still more or less asleep, had spotted Jack. "There's a guy out there with wire rim glasses!" she was wailing. "He's probably a pervert!"

Meanwhile, Ann Donnelly, whose room abutted the door on the other side, appeared. By this time, I was peering in the door. "That's no pervert," she said. "That's Kathie Farnell." She swung the door open as Pam shrieked "He'll kill us all!"

So much for that date, I thought grimly, but then Jack grabbed my hand.

"I'd like to see you again," he said.

My first thought was "Huh?" My second thought was that possibly the universe wasn't as dumb as it looked.

Aloud, all I said as I slid in the door was "Sure!"

Photo Gallery

All photographs are from the author's collection.

Ramon and
Virginia Ferguson Farnell

Granny (Armitta Alford Farnell)
before she cut her hair

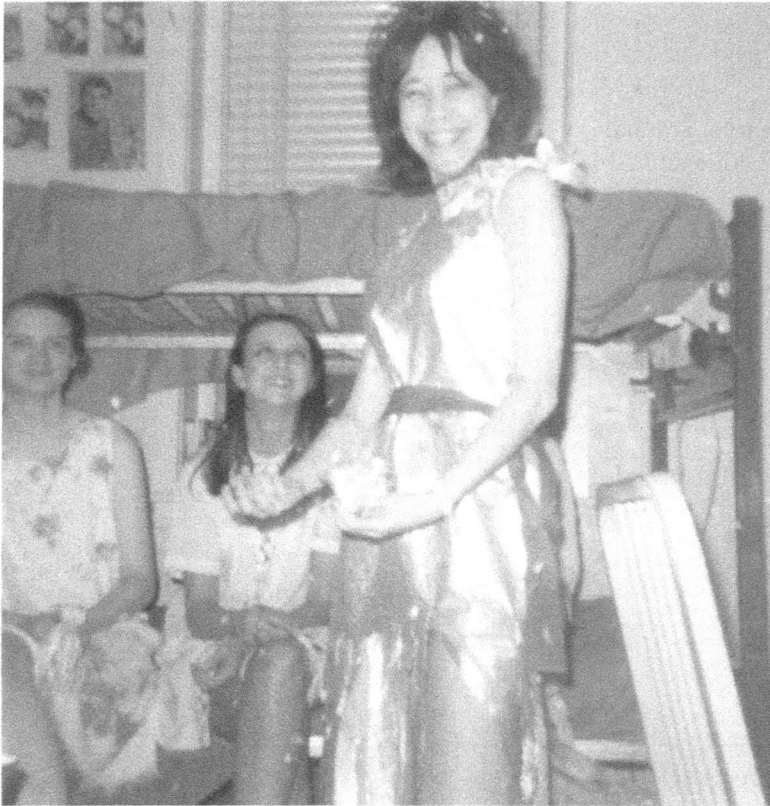

Kathie and the paper dress

Clay at Williams School

High School graduation:
Kathie and Abicat

Kathie,
founder of
the Science
Fiction
Club

154

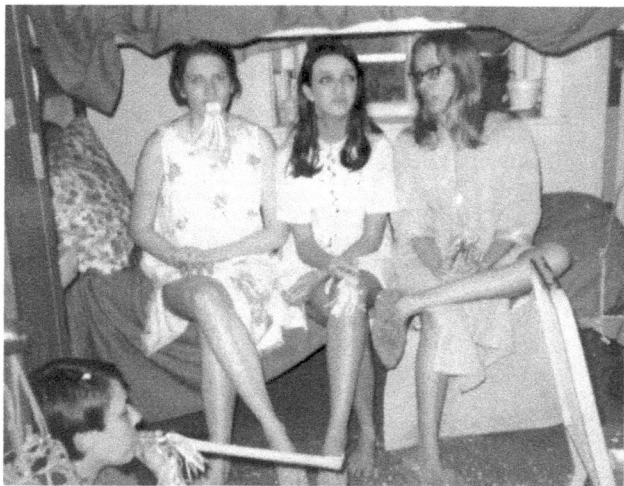

The Montevallo party scene

Summer school in Europe

Kathie working

Mama at book signing

Ray and his future ex-girlfriend

Clay (with beard) and rascals

Acknowledgments

Since *Tie Dyed: Avoiding Aquarius* continues the narrative of events started in my first memoir, *Duck and Cover: A Nuclear Family*, I'd like to thank everyone who enjoyed the first book and encouraged me to write a second. And as usual my highest thanks to Jack, for love and support.

www.ingramcontent.com/pod-product-compliance
Lightning Source LLC
Chambersburg PA
CBHW021845090426
42811CB00033B/2140/J